MONTEZUMA

MILITARY PROFILES
SERIES EDITOR
Dennis E. Showalter, Ph.D.
The Colorado College

*Instructive summaries for general and expert
readers alike, volumes in the Military Profiles
series are essential treatments of significant and
popular military figures drawn from world history,
ancient times through the present.*

MONTEZUMA

Warlord of the Aztecs

Peter G. Tsouras

POTOMAC BOOKS, INC.
Washington, D.C.

Library of Congress Cataloging-in-Publication Data

Tsouras, Peter.
Montezuma : warlord of the Aztecs / Peter G.
    Tsouras.—1st ed.
        p. cm.— (Military profiles)
    Includes bibliographical references and index.
    ISBN 1-57488-821-8 (cl. : alk. paper)—
ISBN 1-57488-822-6 (pb. : alk. paper)
    1. Montezuma II, Emperor of Mexico, ca. 1480-
1520. 2. Aztecs—History—16th century. 3. Aztecs—
Kings and rulers—Biography. 4. Mexico—History—
Conquest, 1519-1540. I. Title. II. Series.

F1230.M6T76 2004
972'.018'092 —dc22   2004006857

Printed in the United States of America on acid-free paper
that meets the American National Standards Institute Z39-
48 Standard.

Potomac Books, Inc.
22841 Quicksilver Drive
Dulles, Virginia 20166

FIRST EDITION

10 9 8 7 6 5 4 3 2 1

To my aunts and uncles, loving fixtures of my life, who have fallen asleep in the Lord—
Katherine, Mary, George, Idell, Dorothy, and Mero

and

Venea, Connie, Chris, and Dorothy

Contents

List of Maps

Preface

Cortés could not pronounce his name and so gave it a Spanish flavor—Montezuma. There was much more about this Indian ruler of fifteen million subjects that the Conquistador did not understand, aside from his name—properly Motecuhzoma, the Angry Lord. But he did grasp the one most correct thing about this mighty man, that he was the single point of failure of his empire, indeed, of his civilization.

Two hundred years before, the Aztecs—or more correctly, the Mexica[1]—had been wandering barbarians before they found their way into the lush Valley of Mexico. There they found civilization, carved out with the obsidian sword the greatest empire North America had ever seen, and built a brilliant capital that ranked as one of the great cities of the world. Mexica armies conquered from the Gulf to the Pacific coasts to the borders of Guatemala. A million bearers carried the tribute of a world into the capital every eighty days.

Motecuhzoma was absolute master of this world, the last of the Mexica rulers to have assumed his throne before the arrival of the Spaniards in Mexico. He was an accomplished warrior and general who added to the endless string of Mexica conquests. To him was due the great efflorescence of this civilization as the wealth of Mexico created a cosmopolitan civilization never before seen in the Americas.

To him also was due the brutal centralization of the empire, withering initiative and flexibility among the Mexica. Always before, Mexica rulers had relied on the good counsel of experienced men. Motecuhzoma kept his own counsel. As the glories of empire mounted, Mexica society lost a vital element of adaptability, the very qualities needed to repulse conquerors from across the sea.

Still, even a rigid structure could well have dealt with Cortés had it been ably led by this autocrat. Instead, the autocrat cracked, victim of his own superstitious nature and a legend of a returned god come to reclaim his rightful empire. The Mexica imperial idea was based on the claim that it was the legitimate heir of the near-mythical time of perfection, the Toltec Empire. Much like the legacy of the Romans for medieval Europe, the Toltecs exerted a powerful pull on the minds of their successors. The creator of that empire, the man-god Quetzalcoatl, had sailed away to the east vowing someday to return. That prophecy had not been an important element of Mexica imperial ideology. His return lay slumbering safely in the ever-receding future, as safely as the Second Coming, until Cortés arrived in the year associated with Quetzalcoatl.

With that, Motecuhzoma was undone. His moral center collapsed. He allowed Cortés to march into his capital and then turned over the empire to him as a god or emissary of a god. The Mexica could do nothing but watch in growing anger and consternation, cowed by the absolutism of Motecuhzoma. The slavish obedience that Motecuhzoma had instilled stayed the hands of men who would otherwise have made short work of the Spaniards. Cortés exploited this weakness to the hilt and through Motecuhzoma's willing collaboration seized control of the functioning empire. The plan would have worked smoothly had not one of his subordinates committed a mass atrocity that broke all the bounds of obedience. But for the Mexica, it was too late. Their victories would be ephemeral, their wounds too deep.

A few words on the pronunciation of names in Náhuatl, the language of the Mexica and central Mexico. Fray Diego Durán referred to it as language of poetry, infinite metaphors, and great subtlety. All words in Náhuatl are accented on the second to last syllable. The *x* is pronounced as a *sh;* the *h* is spoken with a soft aspirant as in English. The *tl* and *tz* represent single sounds. The *u* used before *a, e, i,* and *o* is pronounced like the English *w. Cu* before vowels is pronounced *kw.* Thus, Mexica—may-SHEE-kha and Huitzilopochtli—weets-eel-oh-POCH-tlee; Tenochtitlan—tay-noch-TEE-tlan; Cuitláhuac—Kwe-TLAH-hwac. Many place names were hispanized simply because Spanish tongues could not pronounce Náhuatl words. Cuauhnahuac (Near the Trees) became Cuernavaca, and Tollan became Tula.

Special thanks to my oh-so-talented wife, Patty, who created the splendid maps for this book, and to the family of Keith Henderson for the incomparable illustrations.

Peter G. Tsouras
Lieutenant Colonel, U.S. Army Reserve (Ret.)
August 2003
Alexandria, Virginia

Chronology

1503   Motecuhzoma attacks Tlachquiauhco for its precious tree.

1504   Motecuhzoma challenges Tlaxcallan to Flower War and loses. Motecuhzoma campaigns in the Huaxyacac region of Oaxaca.

1505–1506   Motecuhzoma conquers Tototepec and Quetzaltepec in Oaxaca.

1506–1507   Huexotzinca beat Mexica in Flower War. Revolt in Huaxyacac region suppressed.

1508   Motecuhzoma attacks Huexotzinco, Chololla, and Atlixco.

1509   Failed attack on Amatlan in Huaxacac region of Oaxaca.

1510   Nezahualpilli warns Motecuhzoma of end of their world. Motecuhzoma first sees heavenly apparitions.

1511–12   Revolt of Tlachquiauhco and other southern Huaxcaca cities suppressed. Zapotec region conquered. Flower Wars with Tlaxcallan, Huexotzinco, Atlixco.

1514–15   Upper Gulf Coast campaign.

1515   Tlaxcallan defeats Mexica invasion. Nezahualpilli dies; Texocan civil war. Omens of the end of the world begin.

1516–17   Revolt of Tlachquiauhco suppressed. Mexica are successful in Flower War with Tlaxcallan.

1517   Ship of Cordoba expedition sighted.

1518   Word of the Grijalva expedition received by Motecuhzoma.

1519   Cortés lands in Mexico, 21 April. Massacre occurs at Cholula, mid-October. Cortés tops the pass into Anáhuac, 2 November. Cortés arrives in Tenochtitlan and meets Motecuhzoma in the "Meeting of Two Worlds," 8 November. Cortés calls upon Motecuhzoma in his palace, 9 November. Motecuhzoma gives Cortés a tour of the Great Temple, 11 November. Cortés kidnaps Motecuhzoma, 14 November. Qualpopoca executed, early December. Cacamatzin seized for plotting resistance to Cortés, late December.

1520   Motecuhzoma declares himself a vassal of Charles V, early January. Cortés marches against Narvaéz, early May. Massacre occurs at Toxcatl, 16 May. Cortés defeats Narvaéz, 29 May. Cortés reenters Tenochtitlan, 24 June. Mexica begin siege of Spanish compound, 26 June. Tlatoani Cuitláhuac reigns from June through January, 1521. Mexica warriors stone Motecuhzoma, 27 June. Motecuhzoma dies 29 June. The Spanish depart Tenochtitlan (*La Noche Triste*), 30 June–1 July. Battle of Otumba, 8 July. Cortés invades Anáhuac, 28 December.

1521   Cuitláhuac dies of smallpox, 3 January. The smallpox epidemic ravages Tenochtitlan for two months. Cuauhtémoc crowned, 21 February. The siege of Tenochtitlan begins, 20 May. Cuauhtémoc captured, siege ends, 13 August.

1525   Cuauhtémoc executed, October.

MONTEZUMA

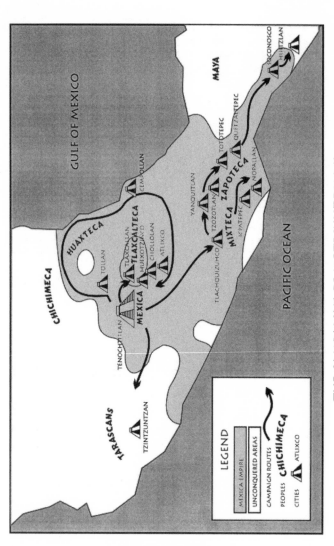

THE CAMPAIGNS OF MOTECUHZOMA II
1503–1519

The Rise of Empire

Anáhuac

In early November 1519 Hernan Cortés and his band of adventurers emerged from a mountain pass and saw the Valley of Mexico, the teeming heart of the Mexica Empire. Known later as the Aztecs, the Mexica had created in less than a hundred years the mightiest and richest empire Mesoamerica had ever seen. Their achievement still resounds in splendor and terror half a millennium later.

What the Spaniards saw was stunning. Snow-covered mountains ringed a valley a hundred by sixty kilometers, home to as many as three million people. Like a string of sapphire blue jewels strewn down its length were a series of interconnected lakes. Rich fields gave way to forests as the land sloped up to the mountains. White cities ringed the lake. This was Anáhuac, "Near the Water," or the "Watery World." The Spaniards' gaze flowed down from the snowy heights to the blue of the lakes to the immense city, Tenochtitlan, resting on islands in Lake Texcoco, connected to the mainland by a web of causeways and nourished by aqueducts. Towering white temples and polychrome palaces glittered in its center. For the Spaniards the effect was more than the senses could bear. They believed they had fallen into the make-believe world of heroic romances and legend.

In a few days the absolute master of this universe would greet them on the edge of this city. His word was life and death, and there was no appeal from or remonstration to his slightest wish. The treasure of an entire world was his, and fifteen million souls did his bidding without question. He was the *tlatoani,* or revered speaker of the Mexica, the descendant of a line of empire builders stretching back almost a hundred years. He bore himself with immense dignity. He was the second of that name and thus was styled Motecuhzoma Xocoyotl (the Younger).

The Imperial Idea

Two hundred years before, his Mexica ancestors had been savages, the last of the Náhuatl-speaking barbarians to wander south from the semi-arid lands of northern Mexico to the lush lake-world of Anáhuac in the late thirteenth century. Despised and feared by the inhabitants for their viciousness and barbarity, they were driven from place to place until they found refuge on the marshy islands in Lake Texcoco in 1345. In a dispute, part of the Mexica broke away in 1358 to form the city of Tlatelolco on the northern edge of the same island group.[1] From the lake the Mexica found a bare subsistence. Of greater value was their warlike nature, the services of which they sold to minor empire builders around the lake. Their last patron was the wily Tepanec king Tezozómoc, who from his capital at Azcapotzalco on the western shore of Lake Texcoco, fashioned an empire in his long lifetime. He had use for first-class fighting men. The Mexica had use for such a patron and tied themselves to him with a royal marriage. In his indulgent dotage, their power grew from vassal to master of vassals. His alarmed successor attempted to destroy them but was destroyed himself, when they organized a great alliance to pull the Tepanecs down in 1428. Their territorial spoils were the kernel of their own empire.

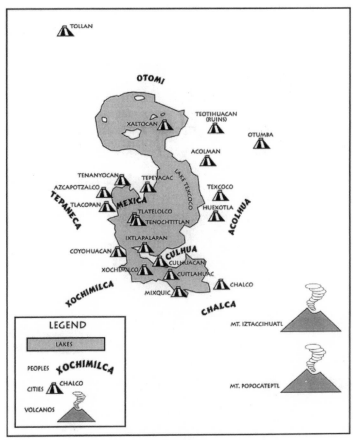

ANÁHUAC:
THE WORLD OF THE VALLEY OF MEXICO

This was the work of a Mexica triumvirate, members of the ruling dynasty of the Eagle Clan. The Mexica *Tlacochcalcatl* (Man of the House of Hurled Spears), or captain general, the seasoned general Itzcoatl, was its leader. He would become the first of the imperial *tlatoani*. The other two were his young nephews, the royal princes and half-brothers Tlacaélel and Motecuhzoma. The Mexica were not strong enough to carry the entire burden of their budding empire alone. Instead they formed the Triple Alliance. One ally was their young kinsman Nezahualcoyotl, king of the Alcolhua kingdom of Texcoco, on the eastern shore of the lakes. Nezahualcoyotl, of the Mexica Eagle clan, had been instrumental in bringing strong allies to the war against Azcapotzalco. Texcoco's place was second in the Triple Alliance. To placate their conquered masters, the Mexica incorporated Tlacopan, a major Tepanec city as the third and junior member of the alliance. Motecuhzoma was advanced to the position of *Tlacochcalcatl* and Tlacaélel as *Cihuacoatl*, literally "Snake Woman," the chief minister.[2]

Tlacaélel was the warrior priest, a man of conceptual and organizational genius as well as a formidable general, diplomat, and strategist. Had it not been for Tlacaélel, the Mexica bid for empire would probably have been no more lasting than those of the mini-empires that had come and gone in Anáhuac over the previous two centuries. Tlacaélel provided the imperial idea, the animating moral force that built a sturdy foundation for conquest and consolidation on a scale never before seen in Mesoamerica.

Shimmering in the past was the memory of the golden age of Toltec Empire with its center at Tollan (Tula), sixty kilometers north of Anáhuac. The Toltecs had engulfed all of central Mexico and were remembered as having brought a time of perfection and unimaginable wealth. Their time remained a golden memory for the peoples that followed.

The burning of Tollan about A.D. 1168 resounded through Mexican history as extensively and deeply as had Rome's fall half a world away, leaving a similar void of order and legitimacy. The fleeing nobility found refuge in many cities in Anáhuac, especially that of Culhuacan, meaning "The Place of Those Who Have Ancestors." Dead though the Toltec state was, the refugees carried in their blood a priceless treasure, legitimacy. So when a miserable nomadic people, the Mexica, entered the Valley of Mexico craving a place among civilized peoples, they were careful to acquire legitimacy through marriage to local royalty of the Toltec bloodlines. They established a monarchy in 1372 of which the first *tlatoani*, Acamapitchli, quickly married a princess of the bluest blood in Culhuacan. From this shrewd policy a philosophy of empire was born, as Tlacaélel boldly appropriated the entire Toltec legacy, proclaiming, in a magnificent exercise of imperial propaganda, the Mexica the heirs and regenitors of the Toltec patrimony.

Tlacaélel's propaganda effort contained another element that was to lay dormant until 1519, when Cortés arrived. Inextricably bound with the Toltec Empire was the story of the founder and author of its magnificence, Topiltzin (Our Lord) Quetzalcoatl. This figure emerges from history in shadowy form as a man named Ce Acatl (1-Reed), after the name of the year in the fifty-two-year Mesoamerican calendar in which he was born. Quetzalcoatl, meaning "Feathered Serpent," was an ancient god even then, and Ce Acatl may have become the leader of the god's priesthood, becoming known by the god's name. Eventually the man and god would become confused in the histories passed down through the centuries. The striking feature of his character was his abhorrence of human sacrifice, then an accepted part of religious life. His nemesis was Tetzcatlipoca, probably high priest of the eponymous god, chief of the pantheon in later times. He was very much a proponent of human sacrifice. Through his conspiracy, Quetzalcoatl was driven from Tollan; he traveled to the coast of Yucatan, where he embarked upon a ship and sailed to the east, in a new fifty-two-year Mesoamerican century's fateful year of Ce Acatl. Ominously, he vowed to return and reclaim his kingdom.

That promise to return did not enter into Tlacaélel's propaganda. It may have even been a relatively minor part of the legends of Tollan. In any case, it survived the burning of all previous histories instigated by Tlacaélel, who was determined that no written account would contradict his vision. From then on, Mexica propaganda would relentlessly proclaim this Toltec vision, at first to eat away at rival claims and later, as the growth of empire achieved a powerful momentum, to disarm morally a growing list of victims.

There was more to Tlacaélel's vision than simply appropriating the mantel of Toltec legitimacy. The Mexica required a far more immediate and constant motive to spur them on to conquest. Tlacaélel was a priest of Huitzilopochtli, the Mexica patron deity, whose name meant "Hummingbird of the Left" (i.e., of the South).[3] Hummingbird was altogether too minor a deity for Tlacaélel's ambitions. The people whose "revered speaker" had donned the imperial blue Toltec cloak and the turquoise diadem required a far more august divinity. Single-handedly Tlacaélel refashioned Huitzilopochtli from a minor war god into the bringer of endless victories. Tlacaélel was more than willing to pay the price. Huitzilopochtli had always been a cruel and bloodthirsty god, but his taste for blood had always been limited by the ability of the Mexica to provide sacrificial victims. Now Tlacaélel provided an increasingly abundant supply of beating hearts. He had struck a bargain with the god—blood for victory. The bargain was based on the belief that the gods required blood to sustain them in their eternal struggle to prevent the destruction of the world. Blood was the most precious of human offerings, the essence of life, and only it could feed the gods. Tlacaélel took things a step farther—blood not only sustained Huitzilopochtli but caused him to reward the Mexica with victories and wealth. So began the cycle of war feeding war. After the Spanish conquest, the Mexica informants of Diego Durán would add that Tlacaélel himself had a taste for human flesh that only endless fresh victims would supply.

Itzcoatl, on Tlacaélel's advice, reordered Mexica society into a thoroughly militarized state. Every male had to prove himself in battle in order to advance beyond the lowest rungs of society. Birth was no guarantee. The greatest rewards in treasure and office went to the finest warriors. Here again Tlacaélel tied the Mexica to Huitzilopochtli, by emphasizing the custom that the successful warrior took captives to offer to the god. There was no premium on killing, as such; Mesoamerican weapons were fully capable of killing, especially the favored obsidian-edged oak sword, but even better suited to wounding exposed arms and legs—and wounds meant prisoners. The thick, brine-soaked quilted cotton suits of body armor were practically immune to underpowered missile and brittle slashing weapons. The efficiency of obsidian as a cutting weapon actually may have inhibited the development of metal weapons that would inflict lethal stab wounds.

Before long there arose a large warrior class for whom war was the road to advancement, and entry to this class was open to talent. War quickly dominated Mexica society. For the ambitious, warfare became a necessity. The Mexica could not, however, be constantly engaged in wars of conquest, known as "arrow wars." Ambition required another innovation. Tlacaélel devised the "flower war," to slake ambition and feed Huitzilopochtli as well. He challenged their enemies to send champions to combat an equal number of Mexica on a designated field; both sides would have the opportunity to show valor and take prisoners for sacrifice.

Despite Tlacaélel's innovations in creating an imperial idea, fostering the cult of Huitzilopochtli, and militarizing Mexica society, the Mexica rulers followed traditional forms of conquest. Unlike the Romans or the Chinese, the Mexica did not incorporate their conquests into a unified administrative system. Rather, on the Assyrian model, the Mexica allowed defeated states to keep their own ruling houses as long as they accepted vassal status and provided stipulated tribute on a punctual and exact basis. This not only eased the administrative burden but allowed vassal rulers to arm, train, organize, and lead their peoples to war. They were often called upon to provide troops for Mexica wars. Nonetheless, a recurrent theme of Mexica history would be a constant necessity to stamp out revolts among vassals who took advantage of any weakness in Tenochtitlan to shed fealty or found the burden of tribute beyond bearing.

Itzcoatl's reign was spent in consolidating conquests in the Valley of Mexico. He was succeeded by his nephew, the prince Motecuhzoma, in 1440. Tlacaélel and Motecuhzoma formed an extraordinarily effective team and together extended Mexica rule well outside Anáhuac. As the twenty-eighth year of Motecuhzoma's rule came to a close in 1468, the brothers could look back with great satisfaction at their lives' work. Tribute and trade flowed in unheard-of amounts from throughout the central plateau of Mexico to the rich Hotlands along the gulf coast, and from as far away as the land of the Mixtec Cloud People in Oaxaca. Tenochtitlan was daily growing in size and magnificence; it had long since outpaced any city in memory. In forty years the two men had transformed the Mexica from vassals so poor their only possession of value was their stolen legacy of Toltec glory, to become the masters of mighty Tollan reborn.

Motecuhzoma wished Tlacaélel to succeed him, but the *Cihuacoatl* much preferred to be the power behind the throne and refused. Instead, over the next twenty years he advanced the young grandsons of Motecuhzoma.

Axayácatl the Scourge

With Motecuhzoma in his grave, Tlacaélel summoned Nezahualcoyotl of Texcoco and Totoquihuaztli of Tlacopan to join him in private in Tenochtitlan in 1469 to select the new *tlatoani*. By custom, Nezahualcoyotl had the right to announce the selection before the assembled royal council, the lords and royal kin of the Eagle Clan. No one could have been more thunderstruck than the nineteen year-old young man to whom Nezahualcoyotl pointed his finger. The Acolhua lord chose Axayácatl (Water Face), grandson of Motecuhzoma through his daughter the fabled beauty Huitzilxochtzin. His father was Prince Tezozomoctzin, grandson of Itzcoatl, Motecuhzoma's own predecessor and uncle.

It was a shrewd choice. Axayácatl thus united the lines of the first two rulers and reinforced the elective nature of the monarchy, opposing any tendency to revert to primogeniture. Perhaps Tlacaélel and Nezahualcoyotl hoped to control such a young man, but if that had been the case, the *Cihuacoatl* could have promoted one of his own sons.[4] Already Axayácatl had, despite his youth, proven an able warrior and had held important junior commands.[5] Perhaps it was this ability and its further potential that the old men had seen.

Axayácatl proved himself an aggressive and valorous ruler. He also had the good sense to be guided by Tlacaélel. His coronation war took Mexica armies to the Pacific coast for the first time, but his first real test came five years later. Relations had broken down between the twin Mexica cities of Tenochtitlan and Tlatelolco. In 1473 he overwhelmed the Tlaletlolca in a lightning attack and cornered their *tlatoani* in the city's temple of Huitzilopochtli. Axayá-catl bounded up the pyramid, engaged him in single combat, and kicked his lifeless body down the steps he had just climbed. Tlatelolco's independence was extinguished; it was incorporated into Tenochtitlan, but it would remain the site of the great market and the home of the far-ranging Mexica merchant class.

Two years later Axayácatl extended Mexica conquests to the west into the buffer land beyond, where lay the Tarascan Empire, centered in Michoacán. Success only whetted Tlacaélel's appetite, and he encouraged further encroachment on the marches of the Tarascans by conquering the few remaining buffer states in 1477–78. The following year, he decided to attack the Tarascans directly. Axayácatl led an army of twenty-four thousand men but was stunned to be confronted by forty thousand Tarascans shortly after his army crossed the border. The ensuing two-day battle was the greatest defeat in Mexica history. For the first time in forty years, Mexica commanders advised retreat. They fled at night, the Tarascans harrying them all the way back inside their own bor-ders. Of the host Axayácatl had brought to battle, fewer than one in ten survived.

No survivor maimed on the field was more crippled than the young *tlatoani* himself, though he bore no mark upon his body. His defeat desolated him. In 1481 he became seriously ill and died, barely thirty-one years of age. Axayácatl was surely one of the tragic figures in Mexican history. Try as he might to follow in the footsteps of Itzcoatl and Motecuhzoma, Axayácatl was too young and unseasoned. His predecessors had each been mature and ex-perienced men when they came to the throne. They also had known how to employ Tlacaélel's genius. That genius, now of leg-endary power, had dominated if not smothered this young *tla-toani's* talent, rather than develop it. Unchecked by the cool judgment of a more mature ruler, Axayácatl had responded to Tla-caélel's bold imperialism with recklessness in pressing the Tarascan War. So crushing was the defeat that it would be over thirty years before the Mexica would seek another war with the Tarascans, against whom they now constructed their only fortified frontier.

Among his many children, Axayácatl left behind a son barely fourteen years old, already known for his intelligence and devotion to Huitzilopochtli. Axayácatl had named him after his own illustrious grandfather—Motecuhzoma, the Angry Lord.

Ahuítzotl, the Lion of Anáhuac

Tlacaélel guided the Eagle Council to appoint Axayácatl's older brother Tizoc as his successor in 1481. As *Tlacochcalcatl* he was the presumptive heir. An able soldier, he was a surprisingly unambitious *tlatoani*. The pace of conquest slowed to a halt. Happily for the Mexica, Tizoc died suddenly in the fifth year of his reign, in 1486, as he was being carried from his palace; blood suddenly gushed from the mouth, and he died. The chronicles spoke of regicide, though no convincing indictments are recorded. Tlacaélel appears to have regretted his support of Tizoc. Perhaps the old imperialist's advice had been particularly unwelcome to someone more interested in gardens than battlefields. The Snake Woman was the ideological founder of the Mexica imperial idea. He had been there at the beginning; his companions had been heroes. Axayácatl had failed in battle, but his valor had washed away defeat. Tizoc was a living insult to Tlacaélel and his life's work, and that life's work was now clearly threatened by the slowing of Mexica expansion. By 1486 Tlacaélel was eighty-eight years old but still lucid and respected. The only one who would have dared to strike at a king was the kingmaker himself.

Tlacaélel threw his support to the last of Motecuhzoma's grandsons, Ahuítzotl (Water Beast), for the succession. The electors of the Eagle Clan were alarmed that Tlacaélel was nominating another young man, this one so young that he was still in school and had not even been to war. So vehement was the opposition that Tlacaélel could not ram his selection through but had to refer the issue to Nezahualpilli, son of Nezahualcoyotl and king of Texcoco. Nezahualpilli had acquired a growing reputation for statesmanship and wisdom, and he had inherited his father's role as the official nominator of the *tlatoani*. He now nominated Tlacaélel, whose refusal was a remarkable indication of his real power: "Have I been nothing? Why have I not put the diadem upon my head, why have I not worn the royal insignia? Have all the orders I have given been null and void? . . . If I could do these things, and I have been doing them for eighty or ninety years, I am then a king and you have held me as such. What more of king could I have been? And it will continue so until my death." He calmed the electors' fears, however, by assuring them that he would act as regent.[6]

Ahuítzotl was literally plucked from school to assume the duties of *tlatoani*. Tlacaélel selected for his coronation campaign the crushing of a revolt by cities conquered by his father. It was an apprehensive army that watched the arrival of the young ruler. Yet the boy proved to be precociously able and valiant, a consummate leader of men, a superb tactician, strategist, and logistician—the very definition of the Mexica warlike ideal. In every way, he was to prove worthy of the titles given by later historians—"The Mexican Alexander," "The Lion of Anáhuac." He wore the insignia of Huitzilopochtli, the first Mexica *tlatoani* to do so. Also during his reign occurred the first blatant efforts to assign to Huitzilopochtli the attributes of other gods, particularly Tetzcatlipoca, the ancient head of the pantheon and rival of Quetzalcoatl.

Ahuítzotl went from one victory to another in the next year, revitalizing the empire's morale and fearsome reputation. Barely a year after his accession to the throne, he determined, to Tlacaélel's joy, to finish the latest reconstruction of the Great Temple. Mesoamerican temples marked the points on earth of divine confluences of heaven, earth, and the underworld. New layers were added to existing structures in ever-greater magnificence to confirm and enhance this confluence. This temple pyramid had two shrines on its summit—to Tlaloc, god of rain and fertility, and to Hummingbird. The temple itself was located within a huge walled compound called the Sacred Square, filled with other temples, shrines, priestly schools, and residences.

The Enemies of the House, the powerful states to the east of Anáhuac, were quick to accept invitations to participate, under safe conduct, in the rededication. The population of Tenochtitlan swelled to over a half million, Ahuítzotl having ordered the entire populations of neighboring cities to swell the crowds of Mexica. He emptied the city's warehouses of a year's tribute to show off the wealth of the empire. Before himself and his royal guests were paraded 80,400 war prisoners and slaves.

The next day the three rulers of the Triple Alliance, dressed in a blinding array of gold and royal blue mantles and loincloths, ascended the Great Temple in the company of the eighty-nine-year old Tlacaélel. Then the captives began to ascend the 114 steps of the pyramid, which took them 106 feet above the precinct floor.[7] Soaring another fifty-six feet into the air were the twin temples. At the top of the stairs, priests seized the captives and bent them backward over stones of sacrifice, arching their chests upward. With practiced slashes, the kings sliced open the chests of their victims, then reached in and pulled out the steaming, still-beating hearts. Blood dripped down their arms as they offered the hearts to the sun and the idols of the gods. Again and again the knives flashed amid red blood spray until the kings grew tired, to be replaced by relays of priests. The killing went on from dawn to dusk for four days in a constant fountainlike spray of blood.[8]

The streams of human blood that ran down the steps of the temple were so vast that when they reached the bottom and cooled they formed terrifying clots. Priests went about gathering this blood in large gourds, taking it to the different temples of the wards and smearing it on the walls, lintels, and thresholds. They also smeared the idols and the rooms of the temple both inside and out, and the stench of the blood was so strong that it was unbearable. It had a sour, abominable smell that became unendurable for the people of the city.[9]

The dead were cast down the sides of the temple to be decapitated and dismembered by deft teams of butchers. Parts of the bodies were distributed to warriors who had taken prisoners, to be taken home, ritually cooked, and eaten as a form of "communion." Ahuítzotl ordered the existing skull rack in the temple precinct destroyed and a new one built to exhibit all the new skulls, now so abundant. Still, the remaining mounds of human flesh presented an awkward problem; it was temporarily solved by casting the headless corpses into the surrounding lagoon.[10] For once, the faultless Mexica sense of logistical organization broke down. The bodies corrupted in the still waters and bred a pestilence that carried off many of the Mexica themselves.

Ahuítzotl had executed a death-soaked propaganda tour de force. He had gathered his enemies in one place, overwhelmed them with the endless riches of his empire, and then stunned them with its ruthlessness. All the time he bore himself with a humble open-handedness toward men ostensibly his equals in kingship. In fact, he had morally disarmed them more thoroughly than had he beaten them in the field. As they departed in silence, Tlacaélel remarked to Ahuítzotl that the memory of what they had seen there would long outlast the treasures that filled their canoes. "Let our enemies go and tell their people what they have seen."[11]

For the next fifteen years Ahuítzotl cut a blood-soaked path through Mexico, taking his conquests boldly up to the borders of the Tarascan Empire in the west and farther up the Gulf of Mexico coast in the east than any Mexica army had ever gone before. He hammered his way through the Mixtec lands and took his invincible armies as far south as Soconosco, along the Pacific coast on the border of Guatemala. No Mesoamerican army had ever traveled so far—a host of two hundred thousand men had marched 2,300 kilometers, and all on foot. Year after year, endless columns of prisoners, loot, and tribute flowed into Tenochtitlan.

The Tlatoani's Nephew

Ahuítzotl consistently had watched the career of his brother's son Motecuhzoma with care. His nephew was only a few years younger, and they may have already been friends. Ahuítzotl saw that the young man had ability and that his reputation as both priest of Huitzilopochtli and warrior grew steadily. The young *tlatoani* was eager to surround himself with talent.

Ahuítzotl quickly arranged a marriage for Motecuhzoma. The bride was a princess from Tollan, of impeccable Toltec descent and great beauty. Every effort was made to find such women for marriage into the Eagle Clan in order to strengthen the Toltec bloodline. Her name was Tezalco; and she was praised for her beauty by poets as the "gliding jewel" of the palace. She would be his Wife of the Mat, his principal wife throughout his life. Though he would take countless concubines and diplomatic wives, she would remain the wife of his heart.

Promotion followed one upon the other. By 1497, Motecuhzoma, at thirty years of age, had proven himself on many battlefields and in councils of the Eagle Clan. He had showed himself an outstanding organizer and an equally good battlefield commander. His advice was remarked upon for its shrewd good sense. Ahuítzotl appointed him *Tlacochcalcatl* about that time and thereby put the turquoise diadem within reach. The position of *Tlacochcalcatl* had often been the final step before the throne. Succession was not guaranteed; the Eagle Clan still considered the position of *tlatoani* to be an elective office, filled from among the most able of the royal kin. In the next five years, Motecuhzoma organized and led in person many of Ahuítzotl's campaigns. Only victory attended his efforts, a record noted by many of the electors of the Eagle Clan.

With office came wealth and privilege. Besides a great residence in Tenochtitlan, he built a summer palace on the slopes above Tollan from which to contemplate the religious and historical importance of his Toltec origins. He built a more comfortable summer palace beyond the mountains ringing Anáhuac in the forests near Chololhán (Cholula). Here again he drew close to his heritage, for Chololhán was the cult center of Quetzalcoatl. The name Chololhán means "the place of the flight"—it had been there that Quetzalcoatl first fled after his expulsion from Tollan. The mightiest pyramid temple in all Mesoamerica—1,300 feet on a side and two hundred feet tall—had been raised there. The structure comprised five temples superimposed one upon another over the space of six hundred years.[12]

At Chololhán Motecuhzoma drank in the stories and prophecies of the Feathered Serpent. Although Tlacaélel had not placed any emphasis on Quetzalcoatl or his return to claim his birthright, the prophecy was a critical element in Motecuhzoma's worship in Chololhán. It permeated Motecuhzoma's sense of the god and devotion to him. What Tlacaélel had passed over, Motecuhzoma took to heart. It was the worm in the golden glory of empire. For all that devotion to Quetzalcoatl, Motecuhzoma had nonetheless become a priest of Huitzilopochtli early in life, following his uncle's example. The conflict he felt between Huitzilopochtli's demand for endless blood and Quetzalcoatl's abhorrence of human sacrifice would surface much later.

Motecuhzoma's office also allowed him to take more wives, but he chose only one more "wife of the mat," another beauty named Acatlan, whose name meant "Besides the Reeds," because her gentleness was like the swaying of reeds in the breeze. She and Tezalco apparently got along well, no doubt because they had separate apartments in their palaces.

Given his nearness in age to Ahuítzotl and the *tlatoani's* good health, Motecuhzoma may well have considered his chances to succeed his uncle slight. When the time came many years in the future, he likely presumed, younger men, perhaps Ahuítzotl's own sons, would bypass him. In 1500, however, the *tlatoani* embarked on yet another campaign, this time to borders of the fabled wealth of Guatemala. Upon his return, he suddenly fell ill with a wasting disease that reduced him to a living skeleton, skin stretched over bones. He died in 1502, still in his early thirties. For Motecuhzoma, in his prime, the turquoise diadem was now within reach.

"There Was Dread in the World"

The Election of the *Tlatoani*

The electors of the empire met to pick Ahuítzotl's successor the day after his ashes had been interred in the Great Temple. As was his right, Nezahualpilli, lord of Texcoco and son of Nezahual-coyotl, addressed the assembled lords. First he spoke of the importance of the office they would soon fill.

> With your vote and consent we are to choose the luminary that is to give us light like one of the sun's rays. We are to choose a mirror in which we will be reflected, a mother who will hold us to her breasts, a father who will carry us on his shoulders, and a prince who will rule over the Aztec nation. He will be the shelter and refuge of the poor, of widows and orphans, and he will have pity upon those who go about day and night in the wilderness working for their sustenance.[1]

Then he spoke of the array of candidates, one of the great strengths of Mexica kingship. "This is the one that you must elect, O mighty lords. Look about you, as there is much to see! You are surrounded by all the Aztec nobles. . . . They are the jewels and precious stones which fell from the throats and wrists of those royal men." Emphasizing the elective nature of the monarchy, he explained that Axayácatl and Tizoc had left many bold and spirited sons, but that if the council was still not sure of them, it could choose from the many descendants of past kings. "Extend your hands, point out your favorite, since anyone you indicate will be a strong wall against our enemies."[2]

The *tlatoani* of Tlacopan spoke next, reminding the council of the need to elect a mature man. The empire had expanded quickly, perhaps too quickly, under Ahuítzotl and could not afford another young and inexperienced *tlatoani*. The early favorite among the electors was Macuilmalinaltzin, Axayácatl's oldest son and Nezahualpilli's son-in-law. He was also the favorite of the military elite. "Popular with his peers and noted for chivalrous love of combat, he was the Hotspur of the imperial court."[3] His nomination fell between the ambitions of the rival warrior caste and priesthood of Huitzilopochtli.

So powerful had the priesthood become that it now openly contested for power with the warriors. The iron will of Tlacaélel was gone from their counsels of the electors for the first time, and for the first time the factions clashed. The forces that he had set in motion over sixty years before were reeling toward a dangerous crossroads. The priests argued that Macuilmalinaltzin did not display the solemn and severe dignity of a *tlatoani*. Even Nezahualpilli argued that priesthood was essential for the new *tlatoani*. For the first time, a sword thrown onto the scales of imperial election did not win the day. In the end, it was the choice of the priesthood that triumphed—Motecuhzoma Xocoyotl (the Younger) eighth son of Axayácatl, and great grandson of the first Motecuhzoma. At thirty-four years of age, he had served brilliantly as the *Tlacochcalacatl*, captain general, in Ahuítzotl's last campaigns.

Motecuhzoma was a bold and spirited commander, an indispensable attribute for a Mexica *tlatoani*, but he was also a high priest of Huitzilopochtli. He stood out even among that small elite with an extraordinary reputation for piety. Ahuítzotl had worn the insignia of priests, but Motecuhzoma was the first priest to succeed to the throne. He had been steeped in the imperial cult of Huitzilopochtli since childhood and possessed a philosophical bent of mind shared by none of his predecessors. As a sop to the warriors, Macuilma-linaltzin was designated next in line of succession.

The messengers of the electors found Motecuhzoma in his own specially appointed room in the Shrine of the Eagles within the Sacred Square. At the moment of accession to the throne, he seemed to match the description of the perfect ruler recited in the lessons of the young.

> The ruler is a shelter—fierce, revered, famous, esteemed; well re-puted, renowned.

> The good ruler is a protector; one who carries his subjects in his arms, who unites them, who brings them together. He rules, takes responsibilities, assumes burdens. He carries his subjects in his cape; he bears them in his arms. He governs; he is obeyed. To him as a shelter, as a refuge, there is recourse.[4]

He thanked his electors with great modesty and with the rea-soned eloquence for which he was famous,

> I would indeed be blind, most noble king, if I did not perceive that you have spoken thus, simply to do me honour; not withstanding the presence of so many fine and noble men in this kingdom, you have chosen me, the most inadequate of all for this calling. I possess few accomplishments required for such an arduous task, and know not what I may do, save to rely upon the Lord of Creation to favour me, and to beg all those present that they may give their support to these my supplications.[5]

He then mounted the steps of Huitzilopochtli's temple with the electors, and in front of the shrine, he bled himself with sharp ob-sidian from ears and legs as sacrifice to the god. By coincidence the day was 14 May 1503, the very day his grandfather, Motecuhzoma I, had accepted the throne sixty-eight years before.

Fangs and Claws of the God

This modesty quickly slipped away in his first act—to fill the of-fice of *Cihuacoatl*, the office from which Tlacaelel had guided the growth of the empire as a shadow king. He shocked the Mexica by appointing Tlacaélel's son, not on merit but because he was in direct line to inherit.

Then he summoned the new Snake Woman and ordered him to dismiss all the palace household of Ahuítzotl. He explained that his uncle had appointed too many commoners to these positions and "that it was undignified and unworthy of a king to be served by lowly people." He was the representative of Huitzilopochtli, and only the finest blood was worthy of attending him. He also wished to teach the sons of the nobility the arts of government.

The Cihuacoatl attempted to remonstrate: "Great Lord, you are wise and powerful, and certainly you are able to do all that you will; but to me it seems that this may be taken amiss, because people will judge that you wish to denigrate former monarchs by undoing their works."[6]

Motecuhzoma was not dissuaded and ordered him to search out the finest of the young nobility to train in the imperial service. He was to exclude anyone born of a slave or illegitimate, even should it be the *tlatoani*'s own brother. The Snake Woman dutifully found one hundred suitable young men, going so far as to measure them all personally to arrive at a pleasing uniformity of height. The young men were instructed in their duties and threatened with death for even the most minor failings. Then Motecuhzoma summarily dismissed all the men raised up by Ahuitzotl—members of his household staff, followed by all the ward heads, royal officials, and captains of hundreds of common birth. Almost as an afterthought, he had them all killed.

Nigel Davies points to two obsessive motivations. Motecuhzoma was extremely sensitive to Ahuítzotl's immense popularity; a cold and rigid man, he must have seen his uncle's charm and charisma as a constant reproach. He also had a stark class consciousness that completely overrode common sense,[7] best expressed in his own words:

> Because, just as precious stones appear out of place among poor and wretched ones, so those of royal blood seem ill-assorted among people of low extraction. And consequently, just as humble feathers do not look well alongside rich ones, so the plumes that came from great lords ill behoove workers and their sons.[8]

However artful his metaphors, the most telling expression of his class attitude was his massacre of the officials and officers of low birth. At one stroke he had destroyed much of an experienced and capable imperial administration to satisfy this prejudice. He was striking at his uncle's memory a second time, as the Cihuacoatl had hinted, because Ahuítzotl had advanced so many men on sheer merit. Motecuhzoma had the pleasure of accepting into his service the sons of men whom Ahuítzotl had dismissed in favor of more capable commoners. He even turned his class attitudes to language; he ordered that only pure Náhuatl could be spoken in his presence.[9]

His actions favoring the nobility may have been clear policy decisions playing one class off against another in order to buttress the power of the *tlatoani*. The rapid rise of commoners under Ahuítzotl's merit policy had disrupted the hierarchical structure of the state. While this argument is surely a part of the answer, it gives too little credence to Motecuhzoma's blatantly megalomaniacal nature and seething personal insecurity. At the same time, his insecurity was evident in his demand to put his immediate environment under absolute control. Everywhere is his insistence on orderliness, routine, and formality. He killed without compunction for the most minor disruptions of this closely controlled world. His attacks on the legacy of his predecessor can be seen as a visceral reaction to a dynamic personality that seemed an enormous threat even from the grave.

Durán recorded another measure when he asked an old Mexica, decades after the death of Motecuhzoma, what the *tlatoani* had looked like. The old man recoiled, "Father, I will not lie to you or tell you about things which I do not know. I never saw his face!" Motecuhzoma had decreed death to anyone who looked him in the face. The same act within his own household was an even greater offense for it was committed in the "house of God." The penalty was death by being shot with arrows or burned alive.[10] His religious preoccupation was clearly leading to a merging of the person of the *tlatoani* with that of a deity. The prohibition to look upon his face was just such an example. Commoners and the lesser nobility had always been forbidden to look upon the image of Huitzilopochtli. Now they were forbidden to look upon the face of the *tlatoani*. Even his seal was carved in Hummingbird's likeness. His status was made all too clear in the words of his lords:

> Although you are our friend and fellow, son and brother, we do not count ourselves as your equal; nor do we consider you to be a man, because you are now possessed of the person, appearance, familiarity of our lord god, who speaks to us and teaches us through you; his mouth is your mouth; his tongue is your tongue; his face is your face; his ears are your ears. He endows you with authority and gives you fangs and claws, that you may be feared and held in utmost reverence.[11]

No other *tlatoani* had dared go so far as to confuse himself with the godhead. It was a fundamental break with Mexica tradition. Although Tlacaélel had been pushing Huitzilopochtli steadily into the upper reaches of the Mesoamerican pantheon for half a century, Motecuhzoma made an enormous leap from that point to assume Huitzilopochtli's earthly manifestation. It was more than a theological revolution. It was social revolution that would fundamentally realign Mexica society. Heretofore, the *tlatoani* had been elected as the best man among a numerous clan of equal claimants. It had been a rough equality that had steadied the *tlatoani* by making them appreciate the advice of men who felt they had the rank and the right to give it. Now that safety check on arbitrary behavior was sacrilege, and its punishment was certain death.

As time went on, there would be indications that Motecuhzoma was not even satisfied with his personal divinity. As his world rushed toward its fate in the next two decades, it was put about that Huitzilopochtli was not just the head of the pantheon, he was the only god.[12]

Imperial Politics

Nezahualpilli was not the only lord who came to regret his support for Motecuhzoma's election, but he was the most powerful. As lord of Texcoco, he ranked second among the three *tlatoani* of the Triple Alliance. He and his father before him had felt a growing apprehension in the overbearing Mexica domination of the alliance. Texcoco, as the cultural capital of the empire, was sensitive to Mexica bullying, and its leading men soon began to form an opposition.

That was evident in the position of Motecuhzoma's brother and rival for the throne, Macuilmalinalitzin, who lived with and had come to identify with his wife's family, the royals of Texcoco. He was the overwhelming favorite of the Texcocan lords, despite Nezahualpilli's support for Motecuhzoma. Support for Macuilmalinaltzin and opposition to Motecuhzoma, especially after his assumption of godhead became obvious, coalesced into the same movement.

Motecuhzoma's attitude to Texcoco was already poisoned. His father had given a sister, Chachiunenetzin, to Nezahaulpilli to tie him closer to the Mexica and to breed his heir. Instead, the young women demonstrated the uncontrollable passions of a Messalina, filling her palace with statutes of the young men with whom she had cuckolded her husband. Eventually, Nezahualpilli discovered her Messalina-like infidelities. As with his father, he would give no privilege to his family but make of them the most painful example to the impartiality of the laws. He would make of it no private scandal but rub it into the nose of the Mexica. He sent the announcement of her trial to every city in the empire and to the Enemies of the House as well. The trial was public and the verdict death. The queen and her lovers were garroted and then burned. Her complicit staff was also executed.

Motecuhzoma and his sons never forgot the public insult but could do nothing for the crime itself was so blatant that even the peasantry knew the punishment. With Texcoco clearly in opposition, he sought other allies closer to home. He had only to look at Tenochtitlan's northern twin, Tlatelolco. His own father had subdued it in the Mexica civil war, slain its ruler, and defiled and closed its temple to Huitzilopochtli. Tlatelolco, however, was the economic heart of the Mexica and the home of its far-ranging and rich merchant class, the pochteca. Their subordination chaffed, and they were eager to exercise the power that their wealth and status as fellow Mexica called for.

Before he departed on his coronation campaign, Motecuh-zoma summoned the lords of Tlatelolco and stated that just because his predecessors had remitted the tribute they owed, he would not. They were lucky he did not demand back tribute. At the same time, he lifted all the penalties his father had imposed on them, allowed them to restore their temple and their status as members of the ruling race. They responded with massive provisions for his campaign and became pillars of his rule. He never remitted their tribute or anyone else's, however. Tribute was a nonnegotiable symbol of submission.

Motecuhzoma now focused on his brother. As his designated successor, Macuilmalinalitzin, would be the obvious beneficiary of Motecuhzoma's own assassination. To move against him directly would sunder the Alliance in civil war. He employed the indirect approach, challenging Heuxotzinco in 1508 to conduct a flower war. He then assigned Texcoco to defend the honor of the Triple Alliance on the designated field of Atlixco. Motecuhzoma had done more than simply challenge Heuxotzinco; he secretly asked them to break the rules of the flower war and fight an arrow war instead. Macuilmalinaltzin led the forces of Texcoco to the field, only to be assaulted by a larger group of enemy, who were there to kill. The surprised Texcocans were overwhelmed, and 2,800 were slaughtered. Two of Motecuhzoma's other brothers were killed in flight, an unheard of ignominy for a member of the royal house. Macuilmalinaltzin himself was captured, but rather than be dragged back to Huexotzinco for sacrifice, he broke free of his captors, seized a weapon, and waded into his enemies with such fury that they had to kill him. Motecuhzoma's treachery could not be kept secret. It became the subject of common knowledge and song. The treachery compounded the utter defeat of a Triple Alliance army, unprecedented since the destruction of Ax-ayácatl's army at the hands of the Tarascans more than twenty-five years before. News of it spread until it rocked the empire and sparked revolts that required enormous efforts to suppress. The news also encouraged the Enemies of the House to band together for a protracted struggle against the Mexica.

Motecuhzoma's strategic vision was cast much lower and remained oblivious to the consequences for the empire. He was entirely focused on consolidating power within the power structure of the empire. With much of his opposition dead on the field of Atlixo, he swiftly moved to crush the rest of it. He dismissed the council of the empire; he would now make all his decisions in isolation, but then when did a god need advice? A purge of officials, generals, and local rulers whose loyalty was in question followed, all part of the ongoing effort to surround himself with only the purest blood. He reached even farther down the social ladder and banned higher education in the *calmeacac* schools to all but the sons of the nobility. There would be no upward mobility to upset the tightly controlled world he was creating.

Nezahualpilli now had much reason to hate Motecuhzoma and bitterly reproach himself for supporting his election. Deep mourning had fallen upon Texcoco after the massacre at Atlixo, no more so than within his own household. His moment for revenge came within months and in the person of Tezozómoc, lord of Azcapotzalco and a father-in-law to Motecuhzoma. Tezozómoc had been accused of adultery; Motecuhzoma had no choice but to have him tried. The judges convicted him but flinched at delivering the necessary sentence of death to the father-in-law of the man who was becoming a god. Instead he was merely banished and his palace demolished. Nezahualcoyotl publicly declared that the judges had failed in their duty and claimed jurisdiction as a ruling member of the Triple Alliance. Tezozómoc's enemies had already decided the judges' verdict had been flawed and added to it by cutting off the end of his nose. Nezahualcoyotl's judges tried him in absentia and passed his death sentence. He was hunted down in exile and killed. At the same time, Nezahualpilli drove the lesson home by sending his assassins to murder a favored nephew of Motecuhzoma.[13]

"He Governs; He Is Obeyed"

Motecuhzoma's exactitude extended to the administration of justice. He was merciless to corrupt judges and was said to disguise himself to hear their verdicts. He was unusually severe in his own judgments. On one occasion when hunting he plucked a few ears of ripe maize from a peasant's garden and then entered the man's house, emptied by the terror of Motecuhzoma's name. He ordered the householder presented to him. When the man had kissed the earth in obeisance, he then straightened up and asked how the *tlatoani* himself was in possession of stolen corn. Shamed by the just reproof of a man normally forbidden even to look upon him, Motecuhzoma removed his mantle, worth an entire village, and draped it around the shoulders of the peasant. The following day, he ordered the peasant brought to him before his court and said that this was the man who had taken his mantle. Calming the shouts of outrage, he explained, "This miserable fellow has more courage and strength than all those here present, because he dared to tell me that I had broken my laws, and he spoke the truth."[14]

A descendant of Motecuhzoma would tell another story. The *tlatoani* frequently went about in disguise to see that the laws were obeyed. On one occasion he left his summer palace on foot disguised as a nobleman to seek quiet in a wood. He heard the sound of chopping and discovered a peasant cutting the wood of a dead tree. The man defensively stated that his family needed the wood, and in the old days it had been the right of the common people to harvest the dead trees. But now the boundaries of the imperial forest were moving ever outward. Motecuhzoma marveled at the man's boldness, for his actions could lead to his maiming or even death. The man went farther and complained that the *tlatoani*'s taxes and labor exactions were crushing and Motecuhzoma himself overbearing in his use of power. Motecuhzoma marveled even more and commanded the man to present himself at the palace the next day. The man's parting words were that he expected no justice at the court but would come. He gave his name as Xochitlac.

He arrived at the palace good to his word and was commanded to stand at the foot of the stairs. He bowed and trembled when he saw a man in the regalia of the *tlatoani* himself descending the stairs. Still, he had the presence of mind "to kiss the earth"—to kneel on one knee, put his palm to the earth, and then kiss it. He then poured dirt into his hair. Only when the *tlatoani* spoke did the man realize that it was the nobleman he had met in the woods. Motecuhzoma kindly touched him and told him to have no fear. The *tlatoani*'s servants placed gifts of clothing and jewels before the farmer. He did not resist when the servants bored through the septum of his nose to place a jeweled ornament and through the lower lip to insert a costly lip plug. The servants wrapped a fine mantel around him and placed a brilliant feathered headdress upon him. The priests ceremoniously painted his face. Then the *tlatoani* called for the elders of the city of Azcapotzalco on the lake shore and presented them their new chief, Xochitlacotzin, his name now adorned with the honorific "tzin," the sign of nobility.[15]

The Coronation War

Motecuhzoma may have been elected *tlatoani,* but his coronation awaited the successful conduct of a war. He decided to wage his coronation war against the cities of Nopallan and Icpatepec to the southwest along the Pacific coast of Oaxaca. These cities had refused to pay tribute, thinking they could defy the Mexica, as did Tlaxcallan. One day into the march, Motecuhzoma ordered the *Cihuacoatl* to return to Tenochtitlan and execute all the tutors of his children and all the court ladies attendant upon his wives and concubines. Snake Woman returned with obvious misgivings but promptly complied with his orders. Motecuhzoma had sent spies back to the capital to ensure that this was done. In these acts, he set the tone for his reign. He instilled fear with sudden and inexplicable executions, tested the loyalty of his ministers, and constantly checked to see if orders had been executed precisely. No remonstrations, delays, or supplications were ever permitted.

Mexica scouts moving ahead of the army infiltrated Nopallan and Icpatepec at night to appraise their defenses. Apparently these cities had erected significant fortifications, something unusual in Mesoamerican warfare. Moreover, his enemies chose not to contest the issue before their cities but to rely on their walls. Motecuhzoma ordered the construction of several hundred scaling ladders. Driven to excel the legendary Ahuítzotl, Motecuhzoma led the attack at Nopallan "decked in plumes so resplendent that he appeared to be flying," and bounded up the first ladder himself and fought his way over the parapet.[16] The army followed him in a rush that flowed over the walls like a reverse waterfall, overwhelmed the enemy, and then thoroughly sacked the city. Motecuhzoma ordered the execution of everyone over the age of fifty, stating that it had been the older people who had led the cities to rebellion.[17] As the lords of Nopallan abased themselves before him, he warned that he would punish any future rebellion with their extermination. The other cities in the rebellious area suffered the same fate. The victorious Mexica army dragged 5,100 prisoners home in its wake, all destined for the stone of sacrifice.

Upon his return, Motecuhzoma rested at a pleasure garden outside the capital but ordered his entourage of kings and generals to proceed. He ordered Snake Woman to receive them with all the ceremony he had set out. When they had gone, he secretly boarded a canoe with six paddlers and entered the city at night. In hiding he watched that the ceremonies were carried out with commendable precision. Only then did he reveal himself.

To his coronation, Motecuhzoma invited the Enemies of the House, and they all came, even the ruler of Michoácan. He entertained them lavishly but secretly, as had his predecessors. This time, though, not even the kings of Texcoco and Tlacopan, his theoretical equals in the Triple Alliance, were informed. The coronation was celebrated with a four-day feast, and each night there was a great dance in which the enemy kings participated. Before they emerged from their apartments, every light in the palace was put out, and they danced only to the shadowy glow of braziers. When they finished to disappear into their apartments, the torches were relit to make the palace glow like midday. On the fifth day, the sacrifice of prisoners in their thousands began. The final event was a mass hallucinogenic party, in which the thousands of dignitaries in attendance fed on mushrooms. After everyone had recovered, the enemy kings departed in secret and under escort, laden with rich gifts, designed for the fancy of each guest. Motecuhzoma thereafter invited his enemies to three great feasts a year. The Tlaxcallans invited him in turn, but he seldom attended in person.

An Imperial Lifestyle

Motecuhzoma's sense of his exalted status demanded that his palace, his "house of god," be more splendid than anything that had ever graced Anáhuac or the farthest-flung corner of his empire. Years in the building, it would stun the Spaniards in its size and grandeur. Europe would not see so imposing a pile for another 150 years, when Louis XIV built Versailles. It probably remains the largest state residence ever built in the Americas, covering six acres.

The palace rose on a great ten-foot platform adjacent to the Sacred Square to the south, bound by canals to the north and west and facing a great plaza to the east. The platform was designed to protect the structure from the floods that had ruined much of the city in the past and to give it a more impressive height. The walls were built of the red volcanic stone of the region, faced and floored in many places with alabaster. The first floor housed the administrative center of the empire and the public places of the court. On the second floor were the imperial apartments.

A set of steep steps led to the entrance, over which Motecuzhoma's coat of arms was inset, an eagle bearing an ocelot in its talons. The vast bulk of the structure was relieved by numerous porticoed courtyards either gay with brilliantly colored awnings or sparkling with flowers and ponds filled with water lilies. Fountains sprayed in the clear air, fed by the aqueduct from Chapultepec, which also supplied numerous baths. Rooms were roofed with wondrously carved, sweet-smelling beams of cedar. Floors were covered with intricate reed mats. The fine plastered walls were bright with paintings or brilliant wall hangings of cloth and feathers. Many of the rooms were immense in dimension, though not of great height. Some were able to accommodate a thousand or more men. Crowds of brilliantly attired courtiers thronged its halls, fragrant with incense. One conquistador wrote that he walked for days on end through the edifice and never saw it all. So vast was the roof that he said thirty knights could easily have fought jousts across it. Fifteen years later Cortés would enthusiastically write to the king of Spain that there was nothing in Spain to compare to it in grandeur and quality.[18]

The residence of the imperial family housed not only the *tlatoani*, his two wives, and their children but hundreds of secondary wives and concubines and their children. One conquistador reported that Motecuhzoma had fathered 150 children. The two principal wives, Tezalco and Acatlan, each continued to maintain separate households within the palace.

Despite the number of children that Motecuhzoma would eventually sire, children had been denied to Tezalco for almost ten years since their marriage. Finally in 1509 Tezalco gave birth to a daughter who would be her father's favorite. "On the fourth day she was named Tecuichpo, and Montezuma consulted her horoscope in the book of fate and found to his surprise that she would have many husbands and would be filled with good fortune. How such a break with Mexica custom could come about was beyond him."[19]

In addition to this great palace, Motecuhzoma maintained numerous estates and specialized establishments in the city itself. One of them was a pleasure palace only slightly smaller than his great palace, faced and floored with polished jasper and filled with balconies, gardens, and pools swarming with waterfowl. Each kind of bird was given its own special environment, and each was fed the foods natural to it in the wild. Three hundred men were required to care for the birds. Motecuhzoma would lounge about the balconies amusing himself at the sight of them. Within this palace was a special room where albino men, women, and children were kept for the *tlatoani's* curiosity. Another great establishment was the imperial zoo, filled with individual structures to house birds of prey and other predators, as well as countless exotic birds kept for their brilliant feathers. Each building was half-roofed in tiles, the other half covered with a fine latticework to allow the animals access to the sun and shelter from inclement weather. Here another three hundred men were needed to maintain the animals.

The most bizarre of Motecuhzoma's establishments was the one "where lived many deformed men and women, among which were dwarfs, hunchbacks, and others with other deformities; and each manner of monstrosity had a room to itself; and likewise there were people to look after them."[20]

Motecuhzoma required his vassal lords to build great homes in Tenochtitlan and spend six months a year in the capital and in attendance upon him. The concentration of so many princely households in Tenochtitlan attracted the creative genius of Mesoamerica in the arts, from architecture to poetry, and transformed the city into a truly cosmopolitan center, the first in

Mesoamerican history on such a scale. Again, he predated Louis XIV, who would similarly keep the troublesome nobility of France in orbit around him at Versailles. Motecuhzoma's purpose was to keep a close watch on these potentially dangerous men and away from their bases of power. Six hundred of these lords were in constant attendance upon him in the palace.

It was an imperial court of the first order. Its food operation was on a massive scale as well, feeding all the lords and their throngs of servants until late at night. Food and drink were available at any time for the lords. Three to four hundred boys were employed in simply serving the food at the great formal meals. Motecuhzoma was served countless dishes at each meal, each hot dish set upon a clay brazier to keep the food warm. A gilded wooden screen was placed in front of him when he ate. He would rarely take more than one bite from each dish and would send portions of his favorite dishes to certain lords as a mark of his favor. "Before and after the meal they gave him water and a towel which once used was never used again."

Motecuhzoma went through four changes of garments each day, each of them a creation of embroidered cotton so fine that the Spaniards would compare them to the finest silk weave. None of them were ever used a second time. Yet, the imitated elegance of his court was to be humbled before the *tlatoani*. Before coming into his presence, his courtiers and other distinguished officers covered their finery with garments of coarse, common weave. There were to be no stars that outshone the *tlatoani* himself. Even these, the greatest men of the empire, were not allowed to look directly into his face but had to keep their gazes low and their postures humble. When he infrequently left his palace, the throngs through which he passed prostrated themselves. Cortés, observing the state in which Motecuhzoma lived in 1519, wrote, "I do not think that the sultans nor any of the infidel lords of whom we have heard until now are attended with such ceremony."[21]

Arrow Wars and Flower Wars

Hammering Oaxaca

The rich Mixtec region of Tototepec along the Pacific coast of Oaxaca had been under assault by the Mexica for several generations and had been much reduced in size. After his coronation war, Motecuhzoma directed his first campaigns there. He led the army in person, determined to excel the now-legendary Ahuítzotl

His first target, however, was chosen more by greed than policy. In 1503 he heard of a small, rare *tlapalizquixochitl* tree, belonging to Malinal, the Mixtec king of Tlachquiauhco. In a land already famous for its fruit trees, the king had imported this tree at great cost for its blossoms, which were of exquisite fragrance and incomparable beauty. Motecuhzoma was determined to have it, even though Tenochtitlan's cold climate was unsuited for such a tropical plant. Nothing of such beauty could exist without his possessing it. Motecuhzoma demanded it of Malinal, who refused. That triggered a Mexica attack. Malinal and many of his people died defending their city, which was annexed to the empire along with all its subject towns. The tree was uprooted and died.

In 1504 Motecuhzoma challenged Tlaxcallan to a flower war.

The *tlatoani* led in person, only to see his Mexica bested. A reinforcing army was defeated as well. Motecuhzoma dispensed with chivalry and led a massive invasion in an arrow war of conquest of Tlaxcallan, which also failed. It would not be the first time he would meet defeat at their hands. Nevertheless, each attack on Tlaxcallan and the other Enemies of the House nibbled away at their dependencies and closed a ring of Mexica vassals around them.

Motecuhzoma restlessly looked to easier opportunities for conquest in the Huaxyacac region of southern Oaxaca near the Isthmus of Tehuantepec; he was brought one by lapidaries and merchants of Tenochtitlan and Tlatelolco. These workers and dealers in precious stones complained to him that the cost of the fine grinding sand and polishing emery from Tototepec and Quetzaltepec was far too high. Accordingly, he sent an embassy requesting sand and emery, for which he would be willing to pay, offering rich mantles. Ostensibly he was asking for an outright business transaction, but the people of the region saw it for what it really was—a demand for tribute—and promptly killed the ambassadors and closed their borders. Other merchants learned of the killings and brought word to the *tlatoani*. He sent other merchants in disguise to confirm the news.

Motecuhzoma mobilized a four-hundred-thousand man army for the 1505–1506 campaign season and marched directly on the two cities. Special commissary preparations were needed because of the huge host and the 1,300-kilometer round-trip distance. A final difficult approach march ended in the face of a river in full flood, with the enemy cities safely on the other side. The force of the river disconcerted his soldiers; their frustration was not helped by the crowds of people from Tototepec and Quetzaltepec who gathered on the other side to jeer and taunt them. Motecuhzoma, who "was the enemy of lost time," was not impressed and immediately ordered balsa wood rafts and portable bridges built. The army crossed quickly at night and was breaking into Tototepec before the inhabitants knew they were there. Motecuhzoma cried havoc as his army rushed through the streets killing and burning until daylight, when he ordered the men back into ranks. Aside from the 1,250 captives taken for sacrifice, only children nine years of age and younger had been spared, on Motecuhzoma's orders. Quetzaltepec also fell.

The next year, 1507, much of the region was in revolt, emboldened by a severe Mexica defeat at the hands of Huexotzinco. The cities of Yancuitlan and Tzotzollan went so far as to send challenges to Motecuhzoma. He gathered two hundred thousand men and rapidly marched them into the rebellious region. From the sleeping city, scouts snatched a prisoner for interrogation. The next day's attack struck the city's weaknesses and collapsed its defense. Motecuhzoma ordered its population put to the sword. The people of Tzotzollan were not slow to react and completely evacuated their city, fleeing so far that the Mexica scouts could find no trace of them.[1]

The army marched on Quetzaltepec again in arms against the Mexica. As usual, scouts moved ahead to reconnoiter the city, but could find no entry through its six sets of encircling walls. The city was now thoroughly alarmed and determined not to try the issue in open battle with the Mexica but to trust to its walls. Motecuhzoma faced a serious dilemma. Quetzaltepec was probably one of the best-fortified sites in Mexico, a daunting prospect for an army unused to assaulting fortifications. Because of subsistence problems, Mesoamerican armies could not sustain long sieges. If he broke off the siege, the stronghold would remain a center of rebellion. The solution was bold, decisive action. He ordered two hundred scaling ladders built. Over three days the contingents from Tenochtitlan, Texcoco, and Tlacopan assaulted the city from three directions. Finally, under a hail of darts, arrows, and stones, assault parties scaled the walls and forced a breach through which the army poured. Only the women and children were spared. Motecuhzoma continued the march through the region, subduing many cities and dragging a growing train of prisoners. The city of Teuctepec alone yielded 2,800 sacrificial victims. Incredibly, the fighting men of Teuctepec left the protection of their four encircling walls to test the Mexica in open battle. The entire campaign stretched over 1,400 kilometers and seventy-four days.[2]

Another campaign was found in the Mixtec lands in the province of Amatlan in 1509, but so many men perished in a blizzard crossing a mountain range that too few remained to bring off a victory. The army's retreat only encouraged instability in an already volatile region. This was the emerging pattern and problem of empire. The Mexica could not be everywhere at once. Defeats or setbacks in one area triggered revolts elsewhere as brutalized vassals grasped at evidence of Mexica weakness. The Mexica were Roman in their relentless hostility to any state that challenged their rule. Defeat or not, they kept coming back until they won.

In 1510 a series of heavenly apparitions appeared over Anáhuac. Their portents spread throughout the empire breeding more rebellion. In the 1511–12 campaign season, Motecuhzoma had to send one army to the farthest reach of the empire, Soconosco, on the border of Guatemala. Tlachquiauhco, once sacked for its splendid tree, was wiped out, the 12,210 survivors of the city driven back to Tenochtitlan. Motecuhzoma's first conquest, Nopallan, was also reconquered, yielding 140 more captives. The Mexica were successful wherever their armies confronted rebellion. By the campaign season of 1514–15, most of these fires had been put out. New conquests were undertaken north up the Gulf Coast, gathering up the last of the Huaxtecs into the empire and even attacking into the barbarous semi-Chichimec lands farther north. The obstinate kingdom of Metztitlan, which had defied his uncle, Tizoc, was fully encircled as well.

Flower Wars Become Arrow Wars

Victories in Oaxaca and elsewhere were paralleled by bitter frustrations in a series of flower wars with the Mexica's traditional Enemies of the House nearer to home. Tlaxcallan, Huexotzinco, Chollolan, and Tiliuhquitepec had survived as independent states in the Puebla-Tlaxcalla Valley through their own strength and the Mexicas' desire to keep them as companions in the flower wars. In the years since Tlacaélel had founded the flower war, Mexica conquests had slowly encircled these states, especially Tlaxcallan. Motecuhzoma evidently believed this tradition had outlived its usefulness. Arrow wars for state conquest now replaced the flower wars for personal prestige. Their very presence was an affront to his increasingly divine self-image as master of the world. His 1504 attack on Tlaxcallan began a conflict that would continue until the arrival of the Spaniards in 1519.

In one of those reversals of alliance, Motecuhzoma made flower war against Huexotzinco, Chololan, and Atlixco in 1508. He called for volunteers, and the cream of the fighting men of the Triple Alliance rushed to join his expedition. Against all custom, he now sent a hundred thousand, instead of the normal small contingent of warriors. To command the army, he picked his own younger brother, Tlacahuepan, who was joined by two more brothers. The three asked for omens, always a risky business for morale. They were all bad. Commending his family to Motecuhzoma's care, Tlacahuepan marched off.

Although the army adhered to the etiquette of the flower wars and committed only a few hundred picked warriors to combat at any one time, the watching masses were clearly applying psychological pressure by displaying the might of the alliance.

Unfortunately for the Mexica, the watching masses were soon having their own morale depressed. Tlacahuepan first sent two hundred Mexica in to meet a like number of men from Huexotzinco. The fighting quickly became a slaughter pen, as both sides forgot about taking prisoners. As the numbers of Mexica shrank, Tlacahuepan sent in a contingent from Texcoco. They too suffered heavily in the swirl of feathers and slashing obsidian and were replaced by the men of Tlacopan. The Huexotzinca also rushed in replacements, and the corpses heaped the fighting ground, "the men behaving like ferocious mountain lions drenched in blood."

Tlacahuepan knew the moment had come for an example. He embraced his brothers, crying, "Behold, my brothers, the time had come to show the valor of our persons! Let us go to the help of our friends!" With a shout, echoed by the battle cries of his men, he led the army into the attack. They crashed into the Huexotzinca with such force that many of the enemy were knocked down, but the Huexotzinca rebounded, held their ground, and called in reinforcements. Convinced that he was already a dead man, Tlacahuepan raged like a crazed lion among the Huexotzinca, driving so deep into their ranks that he quickly found himself cut off and surrounded. Battle madness overcame him. He hacked and slashed at everyone about him until he had left a thick ring of Huexotzinca dead. When no one else would challenge him, he stood still for a moment, and the last of his frenzy drained away in utter exhaustion. "Cease, O Huexotzinca! I see that I am yours and that I cannot defend myself. Let the combat end here! You see me here; now do what you will!" The Huexotzinca rushed to carry him off for sacrifice in their city, but he seized one of the corpses, demanding to be sacrificed among them. They obliged and tore his body to bits, carrying off every piece as a relic.[3]

With their commander slain, the army recoiled. The Huexotzinca pressed hard on them, killed Tlacahuepan's brothers, and captured many lords and captains. As they returned to Huexotzinco in triumph, the Mexica crept silently into Tenochtitlan, leaving 8,200 dead on the field. They were met with mourning and lamentation, and burned their weapons in shame. Then they reported to a *tlatoani* sunk in despair. He ordered their wounds cared for and their nakedness clothed. His brothers he gave a splendid funeral. Motecuhzoma wept and lamented that he did not know how he had offended the gods.

In 1515 Tlaxcallan and Huexotzinco had fallen out and warred against each other. Tlaxcallan, now the stronger party, harried Huexotzinco so cruelly that its king and many of his people fled to Tenochtitlan for refuge, where they were warmly welcomed by Motecuhzoma. He then attacked Tlaxcallan, but his army suffered another catastrophic defeat. Many were killed and captured, and all his chief captains were dragged back to Tlaxcallan as captives. Only eighty Tlaxcallan captives were taken. When this news reached him, Motecuhzoma leaped from his throne in fury and shouted, "What is this you say? Do you know what you are saying? Are not the Aztecs filled with shame? Since when have you lost your vigor, your strength, like weak women? Are you just learning to take up the sword and the shield, the bow and the arrow? What has happened to all the skill acquired since the founding of this renowned city? How has it been lost to the point that I stand in shame before the entire world? Why did so many courageous lords and captains, seasoned in war, go to the battlefield? Is it possible that they have forgotten how to command their squadrons . . . ? I can only believe that they were deliberately heedless in order to mock me!"[4]

The returning army was shown no honors, nor even any signs of mourning. When its leaders arrived at the palace to make their report, its doors were slammed in their faces. Motecuhzoma ordered that they be publicly shamed. Royal judges went to their homes to strip them of their insignia and shear their hair. They were forbidden the right to wear cotton or sandals and to even enter the royal palace for a year.

The war against Tlaxcallan had yielded a single prize, however. Tlahuicoli, a famous Tlaxcallan captain of international renown, had been captured in the campaign. So impressed was he with Tlahuicoli's deeds and bearing that Motecuhzoma put him in command of an expedition against the Tarascans. Their army marched beyond Tolocan and fought a great battle on the Tarascan border. Although they did not retain the field, the Mexica took many captives and much booty. For Motecuhzoma, this battle must have been one of the sweetest of all; it restored Mexica prestige and furthered Ahuítzotl's gradual encirclement of Michoácan. Most importantly, it wiped away the defeat of his father, Axayácatl.

Returning in victory, Tlahuicoli refused the freedom offered him by Motecuhzoma and demanded to be sacrificed on the gladiatorial stone. In the ensuing combat, he bashed out the brains of eight eagle and jaguar knights and wounded twenty more with his feather-edged sword before he was cut down and his heart torn out by the Mexica high priest.

At the empire's core, the struggle for the throne of Texcoco after Nezahualpilli's death in 1515 nearly plunged the empire into civil war. Nezahualpilli had left three legitimate sons but had failed to designate the heir. Motecuhzoma intervened and nominated Cacamatzin, the son of his sister. One of the other claimants, Ixtlilxóchitl, refused to accept the *tlatoani*'s high-handed interference, fled to the mountains, rallied support, seized the northern part of the kingdom, and stood off the armies of Motecuhzoma and Cacamatzin. At this point, Motecuhzoma chose to cut his losses. A determined campaign to suppress Ixtlilxóchitl would have torn the Acolhua kingdom apart and fundamentally weakened a major component of the Triple Alliance. Instead, Motecuhzoma brokered a peace in which Cacamatzin was recognized as king, but only of those cities he held. Ixtlilxóchitl was recognized as the de facto ruler of the rest of the kingdom.

The 1516–17 campaign season saw the Mexica put down a revolt by Tlachquiauhco. The former city of the blossoming tree had refused tribute and was stopping trade from the Pacific coast and Tehuantepec, the great entrepot on the isthmus of that name. That same year, Mexica warriors launched a flower war against Tlaxcallan entirely on their own and were victorious. Motecuhzoma excused this act of initiative, so hungry was he for victories over Tlaxcallan. Motecuhzoma's final campaign in 1518 took his armies in conquests against the Chichemecs.[5]

Among the Enemies of the House, Tlaxcallan, Huexotzinco, and Atlixco, all to the east of Tenochtitlan, had been able to keep their anti-Mexica alliance intact. Only Cholollan, the great shrine of Quetzalcoatl, had fallen under Motecuhzoma's control. It was through this region that strangers from across the sea would march, straight into the arms of the Enemies of the House.

Omens of the End of the World

ALREADY BY 1510 the tight bonds that Motecuhzoma had created to keep his world in place had frayed badly. Repeated campaigns in Oaxaca had not quelled the region's rebelliousness, and repeated defeats close at hand in the flower turned arrow wars were an open shame. One day, Nezahualpilli arrived unexpectedly to seek a private meeting. Motecuhzoma was much surprised; it was not like a lord of the Triple Alliance to fail to announce formally his coming. Nezahualpilli's reputation as a seer filled his words with a sense of dread. He had been shown the future. "You must be on guard, you must be warned, because I have discovered that in a very few years our cities will be ravaged and destroyed. We and our children will be killed and our vassals belittled. Of all these things you must not doubt." As proof he foretold that Motecuhzoma would never be victorious in his wars against Tlaxcallan, Huexotzinco, or Cholollan. "I will add this: before many days have passed you will see signs in the sky which will appear as an omen of what I am saying."[1]

One starry night about midnight a young priest of Huitzilopochtli awoke to relieve himself and saw a great comet that seemed to be approaching Tenochtitlan, "bleeding fire like a wound in the eastern sky." His shouts awakened the city, and all watched till dawn bleached it from the sky. The next night Motecuhzoma waited until midnight to see it. Its appearance filled him with such terror that he expected to die where he stood. He cried out in despair asking if he, indeed, would be the one to witness the ruin of his ancestors' glory, "all that the Mexicans had conquered by their strong right arm and by the valour of and spirit that lies within their breasts?" Clearly the warning had sunk to the bone; his first thought was of escape. "What shall I do? Where shall I hide? Where can I seek cover? Oh, if only I could now turn to stone . . . before seeing that which I now await with dread."[2] Nezahualpilli was not helpful, saying only that he had warned of this and adding that he himself would be lucky enough to die before all this came to pass. In panic, Motecuhzoma ordered all his soothsayers and astrologers to tell him the meaning of the comet. When they could not, he threw them into prison and let them die of hunger.

In 1515 Nezahualpilli died, and the omens crowded one after the other upon Motecuhzoma's fears. Huitzilopochtli's temple atop its pyramid mysteriously burst into flame that not even a frantic bucket brigade could extinguish before the temple burned completely. Then lightning, coming out of a drizzling sky, destroyed the temple of the fire god. Following this, another comet, this one three-headed, plowed across the sky from east to west, hiding the sun. A sudden, inexplicable swell of Lake Texcoco surged through Tenochtitlan, destroying many of the poorer houses. Worst of all, a woman was heard at night, the time of greatest dread, wandering through all the districts of the city, wailing, "O my children, you are lost; where shall I hide you?" This was seen as the goddess Cihuacoatl, the mother of their patron deity, Huitzilopotchli. The news of her apparition shook Motecuhzoma to the core. Other omens, spawned by rumor, flew about the city adding to the rising panic. Motecuhzoma summoned new augers, but they could answer no better than their predecessors. In blind rage he ordered them all killed, and their families as well. Even their homes were torn down to the foundations.

Legends have embroidered Motecuhzoma's increasing panic and confusion. In his pride, he had wanted to surpass his predecessors by the grandeur of his monuments, and now he ordered that a great new sacrificial stone for the feast of the Skinning of Men be carved. After the stone was roughed out, its transportation to Tenochtitlan became a nightmare. At times it seemed to sink roots into the earth and could not be budged. At other times, many times the normal number of men were needed to drag it along. Then it spoke to the gangs, chiding them for their futility—it would never arrive in Tenochtitlan, because of Motecuhzoma's arrogance. "Why does he want to take me? So tomorrow I can be cast down and held in contempt? Let him know that his reign has ended. Soon he will see what is to come upon him, and this will happen because he has wanted to be adored more than God Himself." The stone then warned the workmen that harm would befall them should they try to move it, but their fear of Motecuhzoma was greater. Now the stone moved lightly until it reached a causeway bridge before Tenochtitlan. There it suddenly crashed through the timbers and fell into the water, dragging many of the workmen to their death. At Motecuhzoma's orders, divers searched for the stone but found nothing. Eventually the stone was found at its original site, all covered with traces of the offerings and sacrifices with which it had been covered when it fell into the water. Motecuhzoma traveled there, made offerings at the stone, and wept.

It is easy to see this legend adding to Mexica disquiet with Motecuhzoma. Perhaps a great stone was moved with difficulty only to crash through a bridge into the lake, beyond recovery. Rumor would add the supernatural details and the proximate cause—Motecuhzoma's increasing identification of himself as a god, a great sacrilege. They would also have swept into the story the anger at his arrogance and cruelty. Many would have remembered the lessons of royal virtue taught in the schools: "The bad ruler is a wild beast, a demon of the air, a demon, an ocelot, a wolf—infamous, deserving of being left alone, avoided, detested as a respecter of nothing, savage, revolting. He terrifies with his gaze; he makes the earth rumble; he implants, he spreads fear. He is wished dead."[3]

The stories also embellished a distressingly visible panic in the *tlatoani*, who prepared to flee Anáhuac to escape his fate. He had convinced himself that he could find refuge with Huemac, King of the Dead, in what he imagined to be a place of bliss. Sending messengers, he begged Huemac for refuge. Huemac tried to disabuse him of this fantasy and described the hideous torment of the dead. But the distraught *tlatoani* was insistent until the god agreed to see him. Secretly he prepared for his flight, and on the appointed night slipped out of the city in a canoe accompanied by his dwarfs, beckoned by a surreal light from Huemac's cave. At the same time, Huitzilopochtli awakened a priest and told him to intercept the *tlatoani*. Finding him seated and waiting for Huemac, the priest upbraided him for his cowardice. "What is this, O mighty prince? . . . Where are you going? What would they say in Tlaxcalla? . . . Return, O Lord, to your throne and forget this folly because you dishonor us." Then he stripped the feathers from Motecuhzoma's hair and pulled him to his feet. Shamefaced, he gazed back across the lake to see the light from the cave had gone out.[4]

Fate in Three Parts

One of the bizarre stories was verifiably true. A Gulf Coast peasant had traveled to Tenochtitlan to tell Motecuhzoma of a great mountain he had seen floating on the sea. This was a Spanish ship of the Cordoba expedition of 1517. In 1518 ships of the Grijalva expedition were seen north of modern Vera Cruz. They were met by Motecuhzoma's local officials, who presented gifts of rich mantles and received glass beads in return. These they brought to the *tlatoani,* who suppressed information of the sightings, informing only the Eagle Council. In 1519 another fleet of ships was sighted off the Yucatan coast. This was outside the empire, but Motecuhzoma's spies quickly brought him reports of horses, huge man-killing dogs, and cannon. Relays of messengers sped to Tenochtitlan to report their progress as observed by men perched high in trees.

Apparently at this point Motecuhzoma assumed that here was Quetzalcoatl, Lord of Great Tollan, returning from the east. It was the fateful year Ce Acatl, the year of Quetzalcoatl's birth and of his departure across the sea in the repeating 52-year cycle of the Mesoamerican calendar. Also, major events of years under the

Reed sign were to originate in the east. Shortly after his ascension to the throne, he had built a new temple to Quetzalcoatl, near the Huitzilopochtli's Great Temple. Quetzalcoatl's temple was round, an unusual shape, since as god of the winds, one of his guises, he would find easier passage around it.[5]

With this assumption, Motecuhzoma supplied the third part of his fate. The first two were already on the ships sailing along the coast. One was the Spaniard Hernan Cortés, leader of the expedition, and one of history's boldest adventurers—warrior of great physical and moral courage, dreamer of chivalrous adventures, and crusader. As important, he was an educated man, with a keen insight into human nature that made him both a masterful war leader and diplomat. The second was the Indian woman Malinal, named Doña Marina by the Spaniards, a Nahúatl and Maya-speaking interpreter, given as a gift by the Maya in Yucatan. With her tongue and quick mind, she supplied to Cortés a subtle understanding of the intricacies of this new world. So important did she become and so constant was her presence with Cortés that he himself would be called by the Mexica "Malinche"—master of Malinal.

Motecuhzoma's assumption, then, was the fatal third piece. For by deciding in advance that Cortés was Quetzalcoatl, Motecuhzoma utterly disarmed himself. Quetzalcoatl was the founder of Mexica imperial legitimacy; Tlacaélel's propaganda had claimed that the Mexica were simply the rightful heirs of Toltec glory. That argument was now turned upon them with deadly effect—the originator of that glory had now returned to reclaim his domain from his Mexica caretakers. In Motecuhzoma, the assumption was doubly crippling. It struck not only a ruler already predisposed to believe it by a series of terrifying omens and prophesied defeats but also a man whose rigid nature, priestly education, and innate fatalism combined to dismiss any urge to struggle with destiny. Ancient prophecies foretold, "If he comes on 1-Reed, he strikes at kings."[6]

It is difficult to believe that any of his predecessors, especially, the cold-blooded Tlacaélel, would have hesitated to wipe out these invaders, superstition or not. For Motecuhzoma, the superstitions wove a deadly enchantment.

His dread was not so deep, though, that it smothered his curiosity to ascertain exactly who these strangers were. Accordingly, he sent a delegation to the coast. They bore Cortés two gifts. The first consisted of rich presents of gold and featherwork, including the ceremonial costume of Quetzalcoatl, in which they dressed Cortés. The ambassadors were to observe him closely to pick up any clues that would confirm his identity as Quetzalcoatl. Especially they were to observe if the leader ate the food presented to him. "If he eats and drinks he is surely Quetzalcoatl as this will show that he is familiar with the foods of this land, that he ate them once and has come back to savor them again." The second gift was of priceless intelligence to Cortés. It was the incredible message: "Also tell him to allow me to die. Tell him that, after my death, he will be welcome to come here and take possession of his kingdom, as it is his. We know that he left it to be guarded by my ancestors, and I have always considered that my domain was only lent to me. Let him permit me to end my days here. Then let him return to enjoy what is his!"[7]

The Spaniards ate the Indian food with relish, and Cortés presented gifts for Motecuhzoma—a string of beads and some hardtack. The messengers rushed back to Tenochtitlan to find Motecuhzoma waiting with such apprehension that he had been unable to sleep or eat, moaning to himself, "What will befall us? Who indeed standeth [in command]? Alas, until now, I. In great torment is my heart; as if it were washed in chili water it indeed burneth, it smarteth. Where in truth [may we go], O our lord?" Because the ambassadors had witnessed great events, he had two slaves sacrificed before them and sprinkled them with blood.[8] He questioned them on every detail; the descriptions of the great ship, the white and black men, the huge war dogs, and the report of the cannon only fed his dread. The beads he treated reverently and had buried in the temple of Huitzilopochtli. He tasted the hardtack; he said it tasted like tufa stone. He ordered it placed in a costly vessel, wrapped in rich mantles, and sent to Tollan to be buried in the temple of Quetzalcoatl. His ambassador further reported what Motecuhzoma feared most, that this possible Quetzalcoatl desired to come to Tenochtitlan to meet the *tlatoani* in person. "And when Moctezuma so heard, he was much terrified. It was if he fainted away. His heart saddened; his heart failed him."⁹

He was now in the grip of such anxiety that he gathered his imperial council to advise him. They convened in the House of the Eagle Knights—Cacamatzin, king of Texcoco, and Totquihu-atzin, king of Tlacopan; and his chief minister, the *Cihuacoatl*, and his four senior ministers, who included his brother Cuitláhuac. This brother was blunt in opposing a soft line toward the strangers. Cacamatzin, however, keyed on his uncle's apparent desire and suggested that it was unworthy to refuse to receive the ambassador of a great king. In the end, Motecuhzoma decided that everything, short of war, was to be done to ensure that the strangers did not come to Tenochtitlan. It was a fatal compromise. He then sent more embassies loaded with food and the finest gifts, including great gold and silver wheels of the sun and the moon. He also dispatched a crowd of sorcerers to see if magic would drive the Spaniards away (to no avail). The ambassadors also bore the repeated message not to come to Tenochtitlan because the journey was too arduous and dangerous. Motecuhzoma had not reckoned that the very richness of the gifts would inspire the Spaniards to defy the hardships and dangers to reach the source of such wealth.

By this time Motecuhzoma had essentially surrendered to what he considered the inevitable. He was particularly terrified of the reports that the Spaniards asked continually what he looked like. He thanked his ambassador and said, "My fate has been ordained and the Lord of All Created Things is venting his ire against me. Let his will be done since I cannot flee." He could see what lay ahead. "I beg a favor of you: After the gods have come and I have received death at their hands, and I know that they will kill me, I beg you to take charge of my children. . . . In the belief that I have surrendered the nation to the strangers, the Aztecs [Mexica] will take vengeance on my wives and children."¹⁰ He moved out of his great palace and returned to his princely mansion. Finally, he resolved to meet his fate with dignity, as Sahagún relates. "[Moctezuma] only awaited the Spaniards; he made himself resolute; he put forth great effort; he quieted, he controlled his heart; he submitted himself entirely to whatever he was to see, at which he was to marvel."[11]

As messengers sped back and forth to the coast from Tenochtitlan, Cortés entered the Totonac city of Cempoallan and easily convinced its chief to renounce his Mexica allegiance. Cortés already had begun to chip away at the weak joints holding the empire together. He also lost no opportunity to confuse Motecuhzoma. When five of Motecuhzoma's tax collectors entered the city and pointedly ignored the Spaniards, Cortés encouraged the terrified Totonacs to arrest them. Then he met with the prisoners in two groups, telling each that he opposed the arrest and was seeing to their release out of the great respect he had for their master.

In early August Cortés marched inland, having informed the Mexica ambassadors that he was coming to see Motecuhzoma. Spies reported every step the Spaniards took. The deeds of Cortés began to resemble a god's. He marched into the heart of Tlaxcallan and defeated its armies in open battle, where the Mexica had repeatedly failed. Motecuhzoma had good reason to fear this news; the Tlaxcallans, who had frequently bested the Mexica, had succumbed to the Spanish art of war. The Spaniards, in their wars with the Moors, had developed the finest fighting skills in Europe. Spanish troops fought in an integrated sword and buckler formation, much like their Roman ancestors in the legions. A Spanish line was a deadly stabbing machine, with its steel swords darting into the vitals of its Tlaxcallan opponents each time they exposed themselves for overhand swings of their edged weapons. As the Gauls and Germans had fallen to the Romans, so would the Tlaxcallans and Mexica to the Spaniards. The Spanish advantage was more than just in stabbing steel, however. The Spaniards fought as a team; the Indians fought as individuals eager for the glory of seizing prisoners. They died in enormous numbers.

In October Cortés marched into Cholollan, the sacred city of Quetzalcoatl, with his new Tlaxcallan allies and perpetrated a massacre that horrified all of Anáhuac. Motecuhzoma's panic had spread to the population. Tenochtitlan became a city on the edge of hysteria as this mysterious, divine doom approached. "It was just as if the earth had moved; just as if the earth had rebelled; just as if all revolved before one's eyes. There was terror." The Indian memory of the coming of the Spaniards still carries the ring of impending doom.

> And when there had been death in Cholulla, then [the Spaniards] started forth in order to come to Mexico. They came grouped, they came assembled, they came raising dust. Their iron lances, their halberds seemed to glisten, and the iron swords were wavy, like a water [course]. Their cuirasses, their helmets seemed to resound. And some came all in iron; they came turned into iron; they came gleaming. Hence they went causing great astonishment; hence they went causing great fear; hence they were regarded with fear; hence they were dreaded.

> And their dogs came leading; they came preceding them. They kept coming at their head; they remained coming at their head. They came panting; their foam came dripping [from their mouths].[12]

A final stirring against his fate caused Motecuhzoma to send a delegation to meet Cortés just beyond the Valley of Mexico, with one of his lords impersonating him with golden presents, asking the Spaniards not to enter Anáhuac. Alerted by Marina, the Spaniards saw through the trick and dismissed the false *tlatoani*. One final time he sent out his sorcerers to bar the way with enchantments, and once more they failed. The Indian sources described how these sorcerers encountered a drunken man on the road who told them their effort was in vain. He pointed back to Anáhuac, where they could see Tenochtitlan in a sea of fire with the temples roaring like high torches above the general conflagration as the noise of war echoed across the valley. In terror they fled back to Motecuhzoma.[13]

The Meeting of Two Worlds

A Place Called Xoloc

As Motecuhzoma followed the inexorable progress of Cortés, he summoned the kings of Texcoco and Tlacopan to his palace to be with him when he welcomed the *teules*—the gods. He moaned as he said,

> O mighty lords, it is fitting that the three of us be here to receive the gods and therefore I wish to find solace with you. I wish to greet you now and also bid farewell to you. How little we have enjoyed our realms, which our ancestors bequeathed to us! They—mighty lords and kings—went away in peace and harmony, free of sorrow and sadness! Woe to us! Why do we deserve this? How did we offend the gods? How did this come to pass? Whence came this calamity, this anguish? Why did this not happen in the times of our ancestors? There is only one remedy: you must make your hearts strong in order to bear what is about to happen. They are at our gates![1]

In fear of the corporal gods marching in iron to him, he lost his reverence for the ethereal gods. In front of the kings, the court, and even a large number of commoners, he bitterly reproached them for allowing this to happen to him. Had he not served them well, he cried through tears of rage? To the people massed listening in terror, he howled that he was afraid and begged the gods to spare the poor, the orphans and widows, the children and aged. He sacrificed and bled himself to show his innocence. Then returning to the palace he bade farewell to his wives, concubines, and children.

If Motecuhzoma had finally resolved to submit to fate and come face to face with Cortés, he at least was determined to do so in style. If for nothing else, traditions of Mexican hospitality demanded it. As the Spaniards marched up the causeway on to Tenochtitlan from Itzapalapa on 8 November, Motecuhzoma came to meet them in all the magnificent state of the *tlatoani* of the Mexica. A contingent of one thousand nobles had been sent ahead to greet Cortés at the double-towered, merloned fort at Acachinanco, commanding the intersection of two causeways. This was the point where returning victorious armies were greeted, also the spot named Macuitlapilco (the tail end of the file of prisoners), where the file of victims of Ahuítzotl's mass sacrifice of 1487 had extended. Upon Cortés's "approach each of them touched the earth with his right hand, kissed it, bowed, and passed on in the same order in which he had come."[2]

At a wooden bridge near the entrance to the city, a place called Xoloc, Motecuhzoma's procession met the Spanish column. No one could tell that the slight, serene figure sitting in his litter borne by eight noblemen had been in a state of hysteria only a short while before. Now he was completely composed, as coolly under control as when he had led his armies into battle as a young man. His litter was a glittering rainbow, decked with flowers. The Spaniards saw "the royal palanquin blazing with burnished gold. It was borne on the shoulders of nobles, and over it a canopy of gaudy feather-work, powdered with jewels, and fringed with silver, was supported by four attendants."[3] He was accompanied by two hundred barefoot lords, all more richly dressed than the first contingent met at the fort. They marched in two columns hugging the sides of the road with eyes downcast. He had eyes for none of them; his gaze was fixed ahead of him on the flashing steel armor and weapons of the Spanish and on their horses, trying to pick out the god himself.

At an appropriate distance he dismounted his litter and approached the man who could be no other than the god. Prescott described Motecuhzoma at this moment.

> Montezuma wore the girdle and ample square cloak, tilmatli, of his nation. It was made of the finest cotton, with the embroidered ends gathered in a knot around his neck. His feet were defended by sandals having soles of gold, and the leathern thongs which bound them to his ankles were embossed with the same metal. Both the cloak and sandals were sprinkled with pearls and precious stones, among which the emerald and the chalchiuitl—a greenstone of higher estimation than any other among the Aztecs—were conspicuous. On his head he wore no other ornament than a panache of plumes of the royal green, which floated down his back, the badge of military rather than regal rank.
>
> He was at this time about forty years of age. His person was tall and thin, but not ill made. His hair, which was black and straight, was not very long; to wear it short was considered unbecoming persons of rank. His beard was thin; his complexion somewhat paler than is often found in his dusky, or rather copper-coloured race. His features, though serious in their expression, did not wear the look of melancholy, indeed, of dejection, which characterizes his portrait, and which may well have settled on him at a later period. He moved with dignity, and his whole demeanour, tempered by an expression of benignity not to have been anticipated from the reports circulated of his character, was worthy of a great prince.[4]

As he walked forward under his glittering canopy, his arms were supported lightly by his brother, Cuitláhuac and his nephew, Cacamatzin. Cortés had dismounted when he had seen Motecuhzoma descend from his litter, threw his reins to a page, and walked forward to meet him accompanied by his own captains.

Motecuhzoma watched as the shining god, who topped him by more than a head, strode ahead of his captains and opened wide his arms to embrace him. He did not flinch from this contact, but Cuitláhuac and Cacamatzin moved forward to restrain Cortés from the sacrilege of touching the *tlatoani*. Unperturbed, Cortés grasped Motecuhzoma by the hand in greeting. It was Cortés who spoke first.

"Is this not thou? Art thou not he? Art thou Moctezuma?"

Motecuhzoma replied, "Indeed, yes; I am he." As all his lords and attendants kissed the earth in respect of the god, Motecuhzoma presented him a priceless featherwork flower, personally placing around his neck, as a distinct honor, a golden, jewel-studded necklace and a garland of flowers. Cortés returned the gift, placing a necklace of perfumed crystals and pearls around Motecuhzoma's neck. He was much pleased by the gift and, in the style of a great prince, was unwilling to receive a gift without giving a greater one in return. Motecuhzoma summoned a servant and as a sign of great honor personally hung around Cortés's neck two heavy gold necklaces, hanging with golden pendants in the shape of shrimps.

Then taking him by the hand, he led him to the shrine of the goddess Toci, Our Grandmother, and motioned him to sit on one of the two royal seats placed there. The two men talked through Cortés's interpreters as thousands waited in absolute silence broken only by the sound of the water lapping against the causeway walls. There Motecuhzoma poured out his heart in a speech that must have left the Spaniard thunderstruck. Motecuhzoma was the prisoner of the Toltec heritage that Tlacaélel had formulated as the basis of the Aztec imperium. Now that heritage had doubled back upon itself in a deadly fashion.

> O our lord, thou hast suffered fatigue, thou has endured weariness. Thou have come to arrive on earth. Thou have come to govern the city of Mexico; thou hast come to descend upon thy mat, upon thy seat, which for moment I have watched for thee, which I have guarded for thee. For thy governors are departed—the rulers Itzcoatl, Moctezuma the Elder, Axayacatl, Tizoc, and Ahuitzotl, who yet a very short time ago had come to stand guard for thee, who had come to govern the city of Mexico. Under their protection thy common folk came. Do they yet perchance know it in their absence? O that one of them might witness, might marvel at what to me now hath befallen, at what I see in my sleep; I do not merely dream that I see thee, that I look into thy face. I have been afflicted for some time. I have gazed at the unknown place whence thou hast come—

from among the clouds, from among the mists. And so this. The rulers departed maintaining that thou wouldst come to visit thy city, that thou wouldst come to descend upon thy mat, upon thy seat. And now it hath been fulfilled; thou has come; thou hast endured fatigue, thou hast endured weariness. Peace be with thee. Rest thyself. Visit thy palace. Rest thy body. May peace be with our lords.[5]

Cortés replied, as Marina translated, "Let Moctezuma put his heart at ease; let him not be frightened. We love him much. Now our hearts are indeed satisfied, for we know him, we hear him. For a long time we have wished to see him, to look upon his face. And this we have seen. Already we have come to his home in Mexico. At his leisure he will hear our words."[6]

For his part, Cortés was far more frank when he also stated that he came as the representative of his king to persuade Motecuhzoma to accept him as his sovereign and to accept the Catholic faith. All the time they spoke, the Spaniards were craning their necks, staring at the *tlatoani,* restless on their feet, or mounting and dismounting their horses to get a better look.

Motecuhzoma now led the Spanish through the city in his litter to the palace of Axayácatl, his father. The procession was led by dancers and merrymakers and saluted by delegations of black-painted priests shaking censers of fragrant copal incense, and by the old warriors, now retired from war, in their jaguar and eagle costumes, carrying their shields and staffs. The procession passed magnificent buildings, mansions of the nobility, lining the street into the center of the city, their parapets dripping with flowers from rooftop gardens. Everywhere along the street and from the rooftops, vast crowds had gathered to see the strangers. Their wonder stiffened into snarls of rage after the Spaniards passed as they watched the thousands of Tlaxcallan allies march arrogantly through the city they hated, bearing arms. They knew they had thrown a mortal insult into the faces of the Mexica—carrying weapons into Tenochtitlan was absolutely forbidden.

Motecuhzoma was waiting in the courtyard of the palace to greet Cortés, announcing, "You are now in your own house."[7] He encouraged them to rest after their long journey and then with-

Motecuhzoma as a young war leader rose quickly through his own abilities and the patronage of his uncle, the *tlatoani*, Ahuítzotl, to be the captain-general of the empire. (Drawing by Keith Henderson)

Huitzilopochtli, the Hummingbird of the South, was the bloodthirsty patron deity of the Mexica. (Drawing by Keith Henderson)

Human sacrifice had been a feature of Mesoamerican civilization, but it was Tlacaélel who transformed it into mass slaughter as a vital aspect of the cult of Huitzilopochtli. (Drawing by Keith Henderson)

Nezahualpilli, the son of the Great Nezahualcoyotl and Lord of Texcoco, the second power in the Triple Alliance, came to regret his nomination of Motecuhzoma for the throne and became a deadly political opponent of the *tlatoani*. In 1510 he foretold to Motecuhzoma the end of their world. (Courtesy of the Library of Congress)

The Meeting of Two Worlds. On 8 November 1519, Motecuhzoma greeted Cortés at the place called Xoloc on the end of the causeway at the entrance to Tenochtitlan. (Drawing by Keith Henderson)

"What is that which is being said by that scoundrel of a Motezuma, whore of the Spaniards? . . . We must give him the punishment which we give to a wicked man," shouted the young warrior prince Cuauhté-moc, as he loosed a dart at the *tlatoani*. (Drawing by Keith Henderson)

DEATH OF THE EMPEROR MONTEZUMA.

Motecuhzoma died as his people stormed the compound, as the Spaniards said of a broken spirit, or as the Mexica said, by the hands of the Spaniards. (Drawing by Keith Henderson)

drew to allow the Spaniards to eat a princely meal from his own kitchens. He returned that afternoon and was met with great deference by Cortés. He brought as gifts many objects of gold, silver, and featherwork and as many as six thousand finely woven and embroidered garments. He escorted Cortés into a large room and had two thrones placed for them both. After the usual courtesies, the two got down to their first serious discussion. Motecuhzoma began again with the Toltec preamble that underlay his position as repeated here, not entirely clearly, from Cortés's second letter to Charles X.

> For a long time we have known from the writings of our ancestors that neither I, nor any of those who dwell in this land, are natives of it, but foreigners who came from very distant parts; and likewise we know that this chieftain, of whom they were all vassals, brought our people to this region. And he returned to his native land and after many years came again, by which time all those who had remained were married to native women and had built villages and raised children. And when he wished to lead them away again they would not go nor even admit him as their chief; and so he departed. And we have always held that those who descended from him would come and conquer this land and take us as their vassals. So because of the place from which you claim to come, namely, from where the sun rises, and the things you tell us of the great lord or king who sent you here, we believe and are certain that he is our natural lord, especially as you say that he has known of us for some time.

From the preamble he made the next logical step.

> So be assured that we shall obey you and hold you as our lord in place of that great sovereign of whom you speak; and in this there shall be no offense or betrayal whatsoever. And in all the land that lies in my domain, you may command as you will, for you shall be obeyed; and all that we own is for you to dispose of as you choose.

Motecuhzoma had gone from undisputed mastery of a great empire to pathologically wariness of the pitfalls of his new position of vassal. He was anxious to dispel the negative impression he was sure the Tlaxcallans and other enemies had rammed home.

Thus, as you are in your own country and your own house, rest now from the hardships of your journey and the battles which you have fought, for I know full well of all that has happened to you from Puntunchan to here, and I also know how those of Cempoal and Tascalteca [Tlaxcallans] have told you much evil of me; believe only what you see with your own eyes, for those are my enemies, and some were my vassals, and have rebelled against me at your coming and said those things to gain favor with you. I also know that they have told you the walls of my houses are made of gold, and that the floor mats in my rooms and other things in my household are likewise of gold, and that I was, and claimed to be, a god; and many other things besides. The houses as you see are of stone and lime and clay.[8]

He went on to say that his past efforts to keep them from visiting him had been based on childish stories that had terrified his vassals—that they were angry gods. He could see that they were men like any other. Laughing, he said that the Tlaxcallans surely lied to him that he was a sort of god and that his city was made of gold. Opening his robes, he showed them his bare chest and grasped his own arms and said, "See that I am of flesh and blood like you and all other men, and I am mortal and substantial. See how they have lied to you? It is true that I have some pieces of gold left to me by my ancestors; anything I might have shall be given you whenever you ask."[9]

Despite his fatalism, Motecuhzoma was still desperately trying to make sense of the Spaniards. Surrounded in respectful silence by Mexica nobles and Spanish captains, he spent hours carefully asking questions about the country from where they came, of their sovereign, and especially of the reasons for their presence in his empire. Were they of the same people that had been seen over the past two years off his coasts? He showed a special interest, as might have been expected, of the rank of his visitors. Were they related to their sovereign? Cortés deftly parried these probes. As to their presence here, why, they had wanted to meet such a famous monarch and introduce him to the faith of the True Cross. As to their relationship to the sovereign, they were kinsmen of each other and vassals of their king. Cortés had the uncanny ability to give answers that raised more questions than they settled. His answers can only have left Motecuhzoma more disquieted.

After distributing more largess to every Spaniard, a habit that was quickly earning him the rank and file's affection, he ceremoniously withdrew with these words: "Now I shall go to the other houses where I live, but here you shall be provided with all that you and your people require, and you shall receive no hurt, for you are in your own land and your own house."[10]

This affection would be reflected in the Spanish accounts of the Conquest, making Motecuhzoma a sympathetic and tragic figure. The conquistador Bernal Díaz de Castillo wrote, "His face was somewhat long, but cheerful, and he had good eyes and showed in his appearance both tenderness and, when necessary, gravity."[11] It was an image totally at odds with the feelings of his own people, who would have been stunned at the use of the word "tenderness." What Díaz and the rest saw as tenderness was more likely a fear-induced attempt to ingratiate himself in order to stave off the dreaded fate they brought with them. The conquistador Francisco de Aguilar perhaps saw a bit deeper in his description: "The king and lord Moctezuma was of medium height and slender build, with a large head and somewhat flat nostrils. He was very astute, discerning and prudent, learned and capable, but also harsh and irascible, and very firm in his speech. If any of the soldiers, or anyone else, no matter who he was, spoke loudly or disturbed him, that person was immediately sent out."[12]

Motecuhzoma still oscillated between fatalism and cunning. The advice of his councilors had been divided, and those, especially the priests, who were not as impressed as were others with the strangers, continued to urge a harder approach. These men had long ago concluded the Spaniards were not divine creatures.

Playing on Motecuhzoma's mind was the tormenting possibility that the strangers were not gods or emissaries of Quetzalcoatl after all. Yet if they were not divine, they were not entirely human. The word loosely translated as gods, *teules*, had many shades of meaning. One of them was "god-favored," "invincible," much like the heroes of ancient Greece. Motecuhzoma would test them—at a distance. Perhaps as early as Cortés's entry into Tenochtitlan, he had given orders to kill a few Spaniards near Vera Cruz. The head of a Spaniard was duly brought to him. When it was lifted from the jar in which it had been brought by swift run-

ner, Motecuhzoma turned from it with a shudder and commanded that it should be taken from the city and not offered at
the shrine of any of his gods. Heads he had seen in plenty, but this
one was of unusual size and fierceness, with a great mop of curly
black hair. If he had looked for an answer, he had received instead
an omen of dread in a pair of dead blue eyes.

Nevertheless, during the first week after Cortés's arrival, he
played the humble and munificent host. The day after their arrival, Cortés paid a courtesy call on Motecuhzoma in his vast
palace of red tufa and marble.

From the end of his audience hall, Motecuhzoma advanced to
greet them with more informality and friendliness than he had ac-
corded any Indian of whatever rank. Cortés promptly undertook
to preach the Christian religion, point by theological point: "The
interpretation was conveyed through the silver tones of Marina, as
inseparable from him on these occasions as his shadow." Cortés
was utterly sincere in his attempt to convert the man before him,
but he was oblivious to that man's own equally sincere beliefs.
Treading on the heels of the Spaniard's faith, however, was an unfortunate Spanish sense of legalism. As he finished his homily,
Cortés addressed his Spanish companions, "With this we have
done our duty considering it is our first attempt."[13] Motecuhzoma
had listened politely but now quickly put an end to the theological
lesson: "We have worshiped our own gods, and thought they were
good, and no doubt yours are, so do not trouble to speak to us any
more about them at present." Perhaps it was after this that he sent
the order to kill Spaniards Cortés had left behind on the coast.

On the fourth day, the Spaniards asked to see the great market
at Tlatelolco and the Great Temple. Motecuhzoma awaited them
on the platform of the temple. He sent six priests and two nobles
to help Cortés up the hundred steep steps of the pyramid. The
conquistador contemptuously waved them off and strode up un-
aided. At the top Motecuhzoma emerged from the temple to greet
them, saying politely that they must be tired from the climb.
Cortés replied that Spaniards were never tired from anything.
This utter and complete self-confidence surely did nothing for
Motecuhzoma's peace of mind. For seventeen years no man had
ever been as bold in his presence. Nevertheless, he took Cortés by

the hand and with a sweep of his arm showed him the panorama of great Tenochtitlan, the brilliant jewel of the Americas in its lake-blue setting. If Cortés had not realized the extent of the Mexica heartland before, he could not have escaped it in this breathtaking moment. His men, who had traveled across Europe and even to Constantinople, whispered that nothing they had seen compared with the shining city in the lake. Sixty thousand houses spread across the water, with temples rising in white picked out with polychrome brilliance, grand palaces, the network of canals and bridges, squares, gardens, and markets adding color and relief to the mass. The white stucco surfaces were polished to the reflective brilliance of enamel. The roof of Huitzilopochtli's temple was faced with polished obsidian that flashed in the sun. Across the lake the shoreline was crowded with more white cities, and beyond were fields of gold and green, more cities, and then the wooded, snow-capped mountains and volcanoes. The Mexica coursed through their city in numbers that set most of the Spaniards to trembling at the odds.

Cortés then asked to see the inside of the temples. He and his men were surprised that the walls were not richly decorated but instead were covered with a black crust. Several of the Spaniards out of curiosity scratched through the surface with their knives. Their blades cut through an inch of putrefying human blood. The olfactory assault drove them gagging from the precinct. Cortés was made of sterner stuff. After viewing the great images of Huitzilopochtli and Tezcatlipoca and the blood-encrusted walls and floors, he boldly asked if he could place a cross on the roof of the temple and a statue of the Virgin Mary to show that "these idols of yours are not gods, but evil things that are called devils." Motecuhzoma allowed himself a display of controlled anger that was nothing like the outrage of the two black-clad priests with him. Cortés had touched the one thing he would not surrender: "If I had known that you would have said such defamatory things I would not have shown you my gods, we consider them to be very good, for they give us health and rains and good seed times and seasons and as many victories as we desire, and we are obliged to worship them and make sacrifices, and I pray you not to say another word to their dishonour."[14]

Cortés must have known that he had gone too far at that moment. He suggested that everyone depart. The *tlatoani* dismissed him, saying he had to stay and offer penance and sacrifice for the sin done in allowing the Spaniards to climb the temple, see the gods, and insult them. Cortés descended the 114 steps with a little of the starch taken out of him. A bold determination had taken its place.

The Taming of Motecuhzoma

The Seizure of the Tlatoani

Six days after the Spanish arrival in Tenochtitlan, Tlaxcallan messengers slipped into the compound with letters reporting the murder of the Spaniards near Vera Cruz. Already Cortés's captains had demanded the seizure of Motecuhzoma to prevent his turning upon them. The size and splendor of Tenochtitlan had left them sleepless in fear of just such an event, a fear equally shared by Cortés himself. Then, with the boldness that underwrote his every deed, Cortés coolly announced a visit to the *tlatoani* on 14 November.

With Marina and thirty men he was welcomed into Motecuhzoma's presence. After a few pleasantries, Cortés began to berate his host for a series of conspiracies that led all the way back to the coast, and especially for his murder of the Spaniards. There was no choice but to accompany the Spaniards back to their own compound, where he would be treated as well as in his palace, "but if you cry out or make any disturbance you will immediately be killed, by these my captains, whom I have brought solely for this purpose."

These words staggered Motecuhzoma. His first thought was to deny any treachery. He pulled off a signet and gave it to a messenger ordering the officer responsible for the death of the Spaniards to report to him immediately. Then remembering who he was, he tried to stand on his dignity, saying such a demand could not be given to one such as he. Cortés found his every argument parried by a better one; this was the man who had charmed the electors of the Eagle Clan with his well-reasoned words.

Unfortunately, this time his skill was wasted on the grim captains. After a half hour, one of them broke in and told Cortés in a loud, rough voice, "What is the good of your making so many words, let us either take him prisoner, or stab him, tell him once more that if he cries out or makes an uproar we will kill him, for it is better at once to save our lives than lose them." His growl and body language cut through all the blather. Motecuhzoma asked Marina what was meant. Now this iron woman with the silver voice became a player in the drama. In his own language, she made it deadly clear that he had no choice but to come now or die. She sweetened the choice by saying that all would be made clear once he was in the Spanish compound. "What I counsel you, is to go at once to their quarters without any disturbance at all, for I know that they will pay you much honour as a great Prince such as you are, otherwise you will remain here a dead man, but in their quarters you will learn the truth."

Now he was truly unnerved. Desperately, he offered his children in his place. "Señor Malinche, if this is what you desire, I have a son and two legitimate daughters, take them as hostages, and do not put this affront upon me, what will my chieftains say if they see me taken off as prisoner?" Cortés was obdurate. He must come. More talk followed. Finally Motecuhzoma's spirit shrank to the size of the whisper in which he consented to go. Now the Spanish rattle of iron melted into sweet words of consideration, even caresses for the ruined king.[1]

The man who whispered his own moral death was not the young *tlatoani* who had been first over the wall at Nopallan in the glory of his coronation war. There is a Spanish saying, "He was a brave man that day." Courage waxes and wanes in each man, but weariness and fear devour physical courage, and Motecuhzoma's fears had been a long time simmering. Still, courage comes easier when to the champion of a host in the glare of the sun. Now surrounded by his enemies, fear had eaten him through. There was no courage left. It was a fear of his own making. Within him was self-doubt that all the godlike trappings, all the rigid control, and all the haughtiness could not heal. In this place, fear found a rich breeding ground.

Had he been a different man, he might have died well then and there. Surely every one of his predecessors, even Tizoc, would have. Old Tlacaélel would have taken more than a few of the Spaniards into hell with him. Some men do not doubt themselves; Motecuhzoma's entire rule was built upon doubt. The man who set such a store by his exalted majesty failed that very majesty at the test. That was his own bitter irony; for Anáhuac, it would be a tragedy beyond all measure.

Word of his abduction ran through the palace and into the streets, where crowds seemed to form out of nowhere. The Spaniards had wasted no time in summoning his litter. The stunned nobles who carried it cannot have hurried, and even now Motecuhzoma could have rescued at least his reputation and shouted to his subjects to come to his aid. But he preferred the sham of a now-empty pride and calmly told the crowds he was going with the Spaniards of his own free will. So passed his last chance to die well. Sahagún's Indian informants remembered the great confusion when he was carried across the square. Spanish cannons thundered over the crowds, stirring their terror.

> As if in confusion there was going off to one side, there was scattering from one's sight, a jumping in all directions. It was as if one had lost one's breath; it was as if for the time there was stupefaction, as if one was affected by mushrooms, as if something unknown were shown one. Fear prevailed. It was as if everyone had swallowed his heart. Even before it had grown dark, there was terror, there was astonishment, there was apprehension, there was the stunning of the people.[2]

The Taming of Motecuhzoma

Within the palace of his father, he was allowed to pick his own gilded cage—the suite of rooms that pleased him most. To these were transferred such of his royal household as he wished. Within this cage he picked up the reins of government, now increasingly directed by Cortés. Two weeks later arrived the lord Quauhpopoca, his son, and fifteen captains, whom the *tlatoani* had summoned at Cortés's demand. Motecuhzoma received Quauhpopoca coldly and referred him to Cortés for questioning. Asked if he was Motecuhzoma's subject, Quauhpopoca replied, "And what other sovereign could I serve?" He readily confessed to killing Spaniards and loyally refused to implicate that sovereign; he even went so far, as Cortés himself wrote, to deny Motecuhzoma's responsibility.[3] Now it was up to Motecuhzoma to defend the actions of a faithful subordinate. It was a moment when character mattered. When the sentence of death was read out to the entire party, Motecuhzoma remained silent. Then and only then did Quauhpopoca and his followers cry out that they had only been following the *tlatoani's* orders. It did not save them. They were burned at the stake in front of Motecuhzoma's palace, weapons carried from the Sacred Square's gatehouse armories piled high around them in place of faggots.

Motecuhzoma's silence had bought him nothing but more ignominy. Cortés came to him before the execution to put him in chains while the sentence was being carried out so that he could not interfere. Cortés could be excused for that; fear of Motecuhzoma's duplicity made it a prudent precaution. Yet if Motecuhzoma would not stir to defend his own majesty and the sovereignty of his race, could he have been expected to risk everything for a servant he had already abandoned? Yet, he angrily wept at the state to which he had fallen, grieving for the outraged appearance of majesty when the substance had gone. Cortés recognized a broken and pliant man. After the execution he personally removed the fetters and told him that he loved him much and that he was free to return to his own palace. Even the conquistador Bernal Díaz de Castillo saw the Spaniard's assurance for what it was. Cortés told Motecuhzoma that though he wanted to release him, his captains and soldiers would not permit it. Díaz recounted Motecuhzoma's attempt to rationalize his only choice.

> He answered with great courtesy, that he thanked him for it (but he well knew that Cortés's speech was mere words), and that now at present it was better for him to stay there a prisoner, for there was

danger, as his chieftains were numerous, and his nephews and relations came every day to him to say that it would be a good thing to attack and free him from prison, that as soon as they saw him outside they might drive him to it. He did not wish to see revolutions in his city, but if he did not comply with their wishes possibly they would want to set up another Prince in his place. And so he was putting those thoughts out of their heads by saying that Huichilobos [Huitzilopochtli] had sent him word that he should remain a prisoner. . . . When he heard this reply, Cortés threw his arms around him and embraced him and said: "It is not in vain Señor Montezuma that I care for you as I care for myself."[4]

Well he might, for, as Díaz put it, "The great Montezuma had been tamed." None knew this better than Motecuhzoma himself, who felt the awe and obedience of his people begin to shrink away from him. In response he clung more closely to his captors, hoping to preserve the appearance of his majesty. They were happy to oblige with elaborate courtesy and shows of deference.

Now Cortés began a wide-ranging survey of the empire, sending out teams of observers accompanied by members of the *tlatoani*'s court. They recorded the wealth-producing potential of each province and ordered all gold and silver turned over. At the same time, Cortés was breaking down the system of vassalage that held the empire together, replacing it with a more direct allegiance to the Spanish throne. Hunger for gold drove the Spaniard's to drag Motecuhzoma almost literally by the hand through the city to point out its treasure houses, which they looted. They ripped the gold and silver from every object on which they found it, trampling the exquisite featherwork, embroideries, and mosaics underfoot, tossing it to their Tlaxcallan henchmen, and even burning it in piles.

As his empire suffered the same fate as the city's treasure houses, Motecuhzoma's hold on his subjects frayed badly. His capture left the Mexica and their vassals in a state of political paralysis. Seventeen years of Motecuhzoma's autocratic rule had conditioned an already collective society to immediate and unquestioned obedience, but daily humiliation was more than this race of conquerors could bear. Their bitterness ate away at their discipline. Soon supplies to the Spanish compound began to fall off.

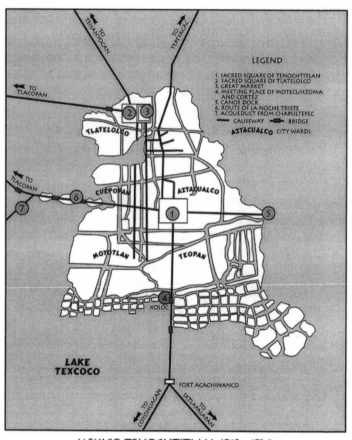

MEXICO-TENOCHTITLAN, 1519 - 1520
(AFTER A MAP BY STUART GENTLING)

From a vantage point on the wall Marina summoned all the Mexica noblemen in the palace and ordered them to bring food, fodder, and firewood to the compound. The first lord to offer open defiance, surprisingly, was Cacamatzin, lord of Texcoco. This king, with a reputation as Motecuhzoma's creature, was in fact a bold patriot. He was the first great lord to reject his uncle's authority. The man whose elevation had been seen as the final subjugation of Acolhua independence now reasserted that independence openly. In response to the orders of both Motecuhzoma and Cortés, he replied, "If we required anything from him we should go and get it, and that there we should see what sort of man he was and what service he was obliged to render."[5]

He was also mobilizing an army. Motecuhzoma attempted to persuade him to visit him. Cacamatzin's reply was worthy of his ancestors, calling Motecuhzoma a chicken for having allowed himself to be captured, "that, when he did visit his capital, it would be to rescue it, as well as the emperor himself, and their common gods, from bondage. He should come, not with his hand in his bosom, but on his sword—to drive out the detested strangers who had brought such dishonour to their country."[6]

Motecuhzoma eagerly offered a solution when Cortés asked his advice. An open move to seize such a great lord would unleash a bloody and destructive war. Better, Motecuhzoma suggested, to seize him by cunning and deception. He had many servants beholden to him in Texcoco. In late December Cacamatzin was lured to one of his palaces at Texcoco that stood half over the water of the lake. There men hidden in canoes under the palace seized him and swiftly transported him across the lake straight into the Spanish compound. He was taken first to Motecuhzoma. The young man's courage had not deserted him, and he berated his uncle for his cowardice. In anger, Motecuhzoma turned him over to Cortés, who promptly clapped him in irons. The lords who had supported him, including the kings of Tlacopan, Itzquauhtzin, and his own brother, Cuitláhuac, were seized one by one and joined him in chains.

Now Cortés held all three kings of the Triple Alliance, as well as the Mexica captain-general. Minor Tlacopan had been in no position to lead. It is tempting to speculate what subsequent course history might have taken had Cacamatzin raised the banner of open revolt and marched on Tenochtitlan. Might the Mexica have gone over to him in a rush and elected a new *tlatoani*? Motecuhzoma's decaying authority would not have survived such a shock. But Motecuhzoma's collaboration cut off that channel of history. Instead, he seemed to accommodate himself to his situation. Cortés even allowed him to offer (nonhuman) sacrifices on the Great Temple, visit his country estates immediately outside the city, go hunting, and sail on one of the recently built Spanish brigantines, although in the company of two hundred Spaniards with orders to kill him if he attempted to escape or raise a revolt. They never had to. He returned happily each day to his cage.

With Cacamatzin safely in hand, Cortés decided in early January to squeeze another concession from Motecuhzoma—a formal oath of allegiance to the Emperor Charles V. Motecuhzoma readily acquiesced and ordered all his vassal kings and lords to assemble to witness his oath. When all the lords were met, Cortés arrived. Motecuhzoma spoke of the Quetzalcoatl legends that foretold the god's return to resume his rule over his subjects in this land. Cortés was his representative, and the time had come to restore his rule. He implored them, tears running down his face as he choked out the words, "You have been faithful vassals of mine during the many years that I have sat on the throne of my fathers. I now expect that you will show me this last act of obedience by acknowledging the great king beyond the waters to be your lord, also, and that you will pay him tribute in the same manner as you have hitherto done to me."[7]

Cortés later observed, "All this he said weeping with all the tears and sighs that a man is able; and likewise all the other lords who were listening wept so much that for a long time they were unable to reply. And . . . that among the Spaniards who heard this discourse there was not one who did not have great pity for him."[8] Such was the drama and pathos of the scene that even the hard-bitten Spaniards wept with him.

Hard-bitten and legal-eyed, Cortés had not studied law in Spain for nothing. He had a notary present to record the event in a formal document, as well as many Spaniards as witnesses to the submission of the Mexica lords. Cortés had unleashed the first plague of lawyers upon North America. Barely had the ink dried on the act of submission when Cortés, in his letter to the king, asked Motecuhzoma to send Mexica escorts with his Spaniards to the provinces and cities of each of the lords and subject princes

> and tell them I demanded that each of them should give me a certain quantity of gold. And so it was done, and all the chiefs to whom he sent gave very fully of all that was asked of them, both in jewelry and in ingots and gold and silver sheets, and other things which they had.
>
> When all was melted down that could be, Your Majesty's fifth came to 32,400 *pesos de oro,* exclusive of the gold and silver jewelry, and the featherwork and precious stones and many other valuable things which I designated for Your Holy Majesty and set aside; all of which might be worth a hundred thousand ducats or more.[9]

Cortés went on to describe the endless treasures in gold and silver, and the countless brilliant articles of cotton that rivaled silk in quality, that Motecuhzoma had freely given him. Of the curiosities that most intrigued him were the richly painted and gold-adorned blowpipes, with golden pellets, a pellet mold, and a gold mesh bag for the pellets.

He did not describe, however, Motecuhzoma's offer of one of his daughters. Díaz tells us the story. "Look here, Malinche, I love you so much that I want to give you one of my daughters, who is very beautiful, so that you can marry her and treat her as your legitimate wife."[10] She was one of the three children he had offered as hostages in his place and had accompanied their father into captivity. Motecuhzoma was simply trying to bind Cortés to him with a dynastic marriage, a worldwide tool of diplomacy. Cortés was immediately aware of the possibilities of such an alliance. He doffed his cap in a gallant gesture of thanks but politely demurred. He explained that he was already married and that his religion allowed only one wife. He would, however, be glad to honor the young woman as befitted her rank as long as she accepted baptism. Motecuhzoma saw no problem, and she was baptized Anna. Within a few months she was pregnant.

"He Had Survived His Honor"

The Gods Have Their Say

Motecuhzoma had surrendered all the things of earthly value—power, wealth, even the sovereignty of his people, almost gladly. Now Cortés would press him for the things of the spirit. Perhaps he felt that this too would follow.

Shortly after the execution of Quauhpopoca, Cortés climbed the 114 steps of the Great Temple with a bodyguard. To let in the light they cut through the thick hangings sewn with bells that covered the entrance to Huitzilopochtli's shrine. They saw the idol encrusted with blood "two or three fingers thick." The conquistador exclaimed, "Oh, God! Why do You permit such great honor paid the Devil in this land? Look with favor, Lord, upon our service to You here."

The cacophony of the disturbed bells brought the Mexica priests. Cortés turned on them and commanded, "Here where you have these idols I wish to have the images of the Lord and His Blessed Mother. Also bring water to wash these walls, and we will take all this away."

The priests laughed and warned him, "Not only this city but all the land holds these as gods, This is the house of Uchilobos [Huitzilopochtli], whom we serve, and in comparison with him the people hold for nothing their fathers and mothers and children, and will choose to die. So take heed, for on seeing you come up here they have all risen in arms and are ready to die for their gods."

Then he turned on the priests and said, "It will give me great pleasure to fight for my God against your gods, who are a mere nothing." With that he picked up an iron bar and leapt into the air to bring the bar crashing down upon the face of Huitzilopochtli. The idol's golden masks flew off. Glaring at the stunned priests, he exclaimed, "Something must we venture for the Lord."[1]

Motecuhzoma, who had been kept almost instantly appraised of the confrontation, sent word asking permission to come to the temple. Cortés agreed and sent a strong escort for him. Accompanied by his captains, he confronted Motecuhzoma when he arrived.

> Señor, I have often asked you not to sacrifice any more human beings to your gods who are deceiving you, and you will not cease doing it, I wish to know that all my companions and these captains who are with me have come to beg you to give them leave to remove the gods from your temple and put our Lady Santa Maria and a Cross in their place, and if you will not give them leave now, they will go and remove them, and I would not like them to kill any priests.[2]

Motecuhzoma was horrified. "Oh, Malinche, how can you wish to destroy the city entirely! For the gods are very angry with us, and I do not know that they will stop even at your lives. What I pray you to do for the present is to be patient, and I will send to summon all the priests and I will see their reply."[3]

Taking Motecuhzoma aside, Cortés suggested that if some accord were not reached, the captains would take matters into their own hands and throw the idols down. After prolonged, tense negotiations in which Motecuhzoma drew upon the full weight of his authority as the earthly manifestation of the god, the priests agreed to the removal of Huitzilopochtli's idol. Motecuhzoma had extracted one concession, that the Mexica be allowed "to take it wherever we wished." Cortés agreed, and "the idols were taken down from there with marvelous skill and ingenuity." With this victory, all the Spaniards ascended the temple steps and heard mass in the section of the temple, washed clean of blood, now reserved for the Virgin.[4]

It was not an accommodation that could last. Motecuhzoma was clearly planning for the restoration of the Hummingbird. He entrusted the idol to Tlatoatl, a loyal servant, who placed it in a hidden shrine in the imperial palace.[5]

Almost immediately, the Mexica priests spread the word that Huitzilopochtli and Tezcatlipoca were abandoning Anáhuac, having suffered an intolerable insult by the placement of the shrine and cross. They would remain only if the strangers were killed. The priests and nobles had been coming with great frequency to confer with Motecuhzoma, who now summoned Cortés to him. With more firmness than he had ever shown in the conquistador's presence, he turned on Cortés his own ploy of blaming others for his own intentions.

> Oh! Señor Malinche and Captains, how distressed I am at the reply and command which our *Teules* have given to our priests and to me and all my captains, which is that we should make war on you and kill you, and drive you back across the sea. I have thought it over, and what seems to me best is that you should at once leave this city before you are attacked, and that not one of you should remain here. This, Señor Malinche, I say that you should not fail to do, for it is to your interest, if not you will be killed, remember it is a question of your lives.[6]

Cortés countered that they could not leave if they wanted to— they had no ships. He suggested that Motecuhzoma give him carpenters to build them, which was readily granted. Cortés secretly ordered the work to be hindered at every point to buy time. Now the Spaniards slept lightly in their armor. He also placed another condition—that Motecuhzoma accompany the Spaniards across the sea to be presented to Charles V. Motecuhzoma was overcome with sorrow at this statement. Yet he said he would order sacrifices, other than human, to be offered to Huitzilopotchli to appease him. He urged the Spaniards now to waste no time in further talk but quickly build the ships.

History was about to be diverted by another character who now walked onto the stage. Panfílo de Narváez had just arrived with 1,300 men near Cempoallan with the express orders from the governor of Cuba to arrest Cortés. He was even able to communicate his mission to Motecuhzoma, who did not inform Cortés. Motecuhzoma's spirits rose. He seemed to shake off his fatalism. Perhaps the gods had sent these new strangers to help drive out the first.

Cortés had no doubt of Narváez's intention. Informing Motecuhzoma that he must leave immediately to identify this new expedition, he left Pedro Alvarado in command of 120 Spaniards. It was a fatal choice. Alvarado was a giant, blond and blue-eyed, ferocious in war, and charming; the Mexica called him *Tonitiuh*—the Sun. It was one of Cortés's few serious mistakes. Alvarado was rash; the man was a killer.

Massacre and War

Motecuhzoma was visibly saddened at Cortés's imminent departure and even offered him a hundred thousand warriors and thirty thousand bearers to help him against Narváez. Cortés politely declined and instead charged him with the protection of the remaining Spaniards, the shrine of the Virgin on the Great Temple, and the property and authority of the king of Spain. Oddly, he had come to feel kindly toward the man whom he had bullied out of his throne.

Before Cortés departed, Motecuhzoma asked of him and received permission to hold the most important of all Mexica festivals, the Toxcatl festival of renewal, dedicated to Tezcatlipoca and Huitzilopochtli. It was always held in the Sacred Square in front of the Great Temple.[7] Motecuhzoma repeated this request to Alvarado, who also approved it, with the provision that no human sacrifice attend it and that no arms be carried. But Tecatzin, the chief of the armories, reminded Motecuhzoma of how the Spaniards had used the occasion of a similar festival to trap and massacre the ruling and military elites of the great shrine city of

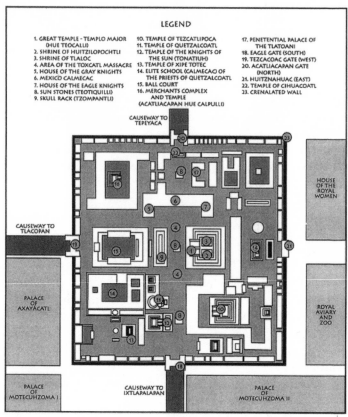

LEGEND

1. GREAT TEMPLE - TEMPLO MAJOR (HUE TEOCALLI)
2. SHRINE OF HUITZILOPOCHTLI
3. SHRINE OF TLALOC
4. AREA OF THE TOXCATL MASSACRE
5. HOUSE OF THE GRAY KNIGHTS
6. MEXICO CALMECAC
7. HOUSE OF THE EAGLE KNIGHTS
8. SUN STONES (TEOTIQUILLI)
9. SKULL RACK (TZOMPANTLI)

10. TEMPLE OF TEZCATLIPOCA
11. TEMPLE OF QUETZALCOATL
12. TEMPLE OF THE KNIGHTS OF THE SUN (TONATIUH)
13. TEMPLE OF XIPE TOTEC
14. ELITE SCHOOL (CALMECAC) OF THE PRIESTS OF QUETZALCOATL
15. BALL COURT
16. MERCHANTS COMPLEX AND TEMPLE (ACATLIACAPAN HUE CALPULLI)

17. PENETENTIAL PALACE OF THE TLATOANI
18. EAGLE GATE (SOUTH)
19. TEZCACOAC GATE (WEST)
20. ACATLIACAPAN GATE (NORTH)
21. HUITZNAHUAC (EAST)
22. TEMPLE OF CIHUACOATL
23. CRENALATED WALL

CAUSEWAY TO TEPEYACA

HOUSE OF THE ROYAL WOMEN

CAUSEWAY TO TLACOPAN

ROYAL AVIARY AND ZOO

PALACE OF AXAYACATL

PALACE OF MOTECUHZOMA I

CAUSEWAY TO IXTLAPALAPAN

PALACE OF MOTECUHZOMA II

THE SACRED SQUARE OF TENOCHTITLAN
(AFTER A MODEL BY SCOTT GENTLING)

Cholollan in the patio enclosure of their temple complex. He urged the *tlatoani* to approve the storing of weapons near at hand. But Motecuhzoma asked rhetorically, "Are we at war with them? I tell you, we can trust them." Tecatzin could only obey.[8]

It had been a priceless warning. Alvarado panicked after first approving the festival. His fears were egged on by the Tlaxcallans, who hated the Toxcatl because so many of their people had been sacrificed at it in the past. Now Alvarado saw a Mexica plot to murder them all in every preparation for the festival.

On the morning of the dance, on 16 May, Motecuhzoma addressed Alvarado, "Please hear me, my lord. We beg your permission to begin the fiesta of our god."

Alvarado replied warmly, "Let it begin. We shall be here to watch it."

The flower of the Mexica nobility and its most seasoned young warriors now streamed into the Sacred Square, completely unarmed, eager to show themselves and their most sacred dances to the Spaniards. The dance commenced in the large open square in front of the Great Temple and the Temple of Tezcatlipoca. Bound by the south gate, *calpulli* (school) buildings, the skull rack, and a few other temples, the area was easily sealed off. Durán states that Cortés had earlier requested Motecuhzoma to summon the cream of the Mexica nobility and the most courageous men to show themselves at the festival.[9] As many as eight hundred of the young seasoned warriors danced to the music of the *huehuetl* and *teponaztli* drums, flutes, fifes, and conch shell horns, as several thousand more clapped and sang in accompaniment. The seasoned warriors were the elite of the Mexica; each had taken four or more prisoners in hand-to-hand combat and wore the most prized of all military insignia, the long lip-plugs and the headbands with eagle-feather tassels.[10] For brief moments as the dance line wound through the square, a shimmering snake of color and movement, "the singing resounded like waves breaking," and the full splendor of Mexica glory unfolded.

The Mexica had not paid much attention to the Spaniards and Tlaxcallans assembling at the gate and around the dance area, closing off escape. As the dance reached a crescendo of ecstasy, the Mexica did not hear Alvarado shout, *"Mueran!"* ("Let them die!").

The first to die was the young dancer who led the great procession. The next were the priest drummers. A Spaniard leaped forward and sliced off an old man's hands; as he staggered back stunned, his stumps spurting blood, the next blow sent his head tumbling onto the flagstones. Now the slaughter became general as the Spaniards and Tlaxcallans converged on the dancers. Sahagún records it vividly.

> Then they all pierced the people with iron lances and they struck them each with iron swords. Of some they slashed open their backs: then their entrails gushed out. Of some they cut their heads; their heads were absolutely pulverized. And some they struck on the shoulder; they split openings. . . . Of some they struck repeatedly the shanks; of some. the thighs; of some the belly; then their entrails gushed forth. And when in vain one would run he would only drag his intestines like something raw as he tried to escape. Nowhere could he go.[11]

When they had butchered the dancers, the Spaniards and Tlaxcallans turned on the crowd. Some bravely and futilely tried to defend themselves with pine staves. Most died. Durán wrote, "The dreadful screams and lamentations in that patio! And no one there to aid them!"[12] Some climbed over the walls, others feigned death in the heaps of corpses, while others fled to hide in the surrounding temple buildings, where the Spaniards pursued them. Blood pooled across the polished flagstones of the square raising a great stench. While this was going on, other Spaniards killed almost all of Motecuhzoma's attendants and most of the imprisoned lords.

The Mexica had suffered a national calamity. Alvarado had massacred much of the military and political leadership of the empire in one bloody hour. Most of the experienced military commanders at all levels, from leaders of armies to the seasoned warriors whose experience steadied the ranks, were dead. The few bloodied survivors fled out of the now unguarded gates and over the walls to disperse into the city with their tale of horror. A priest shouted the alarm. "O brave warriors, O Mexicans, hasten here! Let there be arraying—the devices, the shields, the arrows! Come! Hasten here! Already they have died, they have perished, they have been annihilated, O Mexicans, O brave warriors!"[13]

The city now erupted in a wild, roaring frenzy; men rushed to the armories to arm themselves as the few surviving leaders sounded the tocsin. Alvarado's men had cut their way to the top of the Great Temple and murdered all the priests. As they tried to make their way back to their compound, they met the unorganized fury of the Mexica, who rushed upon them freshly armed. Other men had rushed to the temple, littered with its dead priests, to beat the great throbbing snakeskin drums to rouse the city. The Spaniards fought desperately through the hacking press back to the compound, pursued by sheets of missiles so thick "it was as if a mass of deep yellow reeds spread over the Spaniards."[14]

Alvarado stormed into Motecuhzoma's rooms, his head streaming blood from a sling stone. He shouted for the *tlatoani* to see what his people had done to him—this, as the blood of Motecuhzoma's attendants still lay fresh on the floor. Motecuhzoma would not cringe. "Alvarado, if you had not begun it, my men would not have done this. You have ruined yourselves and me also."[15] Alvarado's attention quickly turned to the mass of Mexica warriors attempting to storm the compound. The situation became so desperate, even with the help of several thousand Tlaxcallans, that Alvarado rushed back to Motecuhzoma and put a knife to his chest, ordering him to call off the storm. Accompanied by Itzquauhtzin, lord of Tlatelolco, he climbed to the roof and spoke, saying to his people that they were unequal to the Spaniards and to cease fighting. "Let the arrow and shield be stilled," he ordered.

A bold warrior cried out, "What is he saying, this whore of the Spaniards?"[16] But slowly the angry crowds of warriors broke up and left the square. Motecuhzoma had used the last of his authority. From that day onward, he was no longer the *tlatoani*. But the Mexica had not yet found a successor.

As the days passed, the Spaniards could hear the keening and lamentation of a city in mourning. Sporadic fighting continued here and there, but no more assaults struck the compound. The bridges over the canals were taken up, and the canals were dredged and deepened, and their sides made steep. It became death for a Mexica to deliver food to the compound. Those who had actively supported the Spaniards were hunted down and killed. With

Motecuhzoma discredited and most who could have replaced him murdered, the situation hung in limbo.

Perhaps what forced Motecuhzoma to climb to the roof that day was a report that Cortés had defeated Narváez on 29 May and was returning with both armies under his command. Outside Texcoco, Motecuhzoma's envoys related Alvarado's outrage to the conquistador. When Cortés entered the city on 24 June, it was deathly silent, with not an inhabitant to be seen. The people had hidden themselves, under the orders of their war leaders. It must have raised the hackles on the backs of the Spaniards' necks to march through that eerily silent city. Cortés was beside himself with anger. He had bragged to Narváez's men that he held the empire and its capital in the palm of his hand. Now he was greeted with news of disaster amidst a shrieking silence.

The fury that he could not turn on Alvarado, whom he would need in the coming fighting,[17] he turned on Motecuhzoma, snubbing him when the Mexica tried to greet him in the courtyard upon his return. He had learned during his expedition that Motecuhzoma had communicated secretly with Narváez to effect Cortés's arrest and his own liberation.

He was in an even worse state of mind when Motecuhzoma requested Cortés to call upon him. He shouted, "Go to, for a dog, who will not even keep open a market, and does not order food to be given us." He even turned away a son that Motecuhzoma sent to smooth the way.

According to Díaz, his captains immediately remonstrated with him, exclaiming, "Señor, moderate your anger and reflect how much good and honour this king of these countries has done us, who is so good that had it not been for him we should all of us be dead, and they would have eaten us, and remember that he has even given you his daughters."[18]

Their arguments brought the ever-practical Cortés to his senses. Resupply was vital. All deliveries of food had stopped before Cortés had even arrived in the city with his large reinforcement. He asked Motecuhzoma to order the resumption of deliveries. Motecuhzoma in turn made it clear that the only officials who could order and organize such an undertaking were locked up with him. He must send someone. Almost absentmindedly, Cortés said to send anyone he wanted. Motecuhzoma chose Cuitláhuac, his brother.

Cortés agreed, and Cuitláhuac walked out through the palace gate. He was greeted by Cuauhtémoc, the twenty-five-year-old son of Ahuítzotl. His name meant "falling eagle," a metaphor for the dusk. Motecuhzoma had early marked his nephew, a fiery young warrior prince, for great things. For his record on the battlefield, he had already made him a lord of Tlatelolco and had given him as a mark of esteem a daughter, Xuchimatzatzin, as wife, before the arrival of the Spaniards. They already had several children. Cuauhtémoc was a man of initiative and had organized the resistance, but he was delighted to see Cuitláhuac, who was next in line for succession as the able and experienced *tlacochcalcatl*, the captain-general of the empire. A special council was convened to appoint him *tlatoani*. The usual elaborate gathering of the imperial electors, flowery speeches, and endless ceremonial went by the board. Action was urgent. He immediately met the desperate Mexica need for leadership. The Mexica at last had a bold and determined leader, a warlord. Already they had been preparing for war, but Cuitláhuac supplied three vital elements: the firm unity of command that quickly brought order and efficiency to the preparations; the plan of operations to destroy the criminals in the Palace of Axayácatl; and the political direction and will to fight to the finish. There would be no negotiations.

Cuitláhuac now made sure that Cortés did not have much time to worry about Motecuhzoma. On 26 June the latter's erstwhile subjects suddenly appeared in vast numbers to assault the compound. The days passed in ferocious fighting stopped only by the coming of night. The Spaniards found themselves in ever more desperate straits, as Mexica assault parties fought for lodgments on the walls while other parties sapped the walls or smashed at the gates with improvised battering rams. Cortés clearly saw that it was only a matter of time before the Mexica overwhelmed them. He needed peace desperately and was willing to sue for it. During a lull in the fighting, he pointed out a group of brilliantly arrayed Mexica on a nearby building. The chief of them stood out in his splendid panoply, and Cortés asked who it was. Motecuhzoma replied calmly that the warrior was his brother.

The fighting went on. The Spanish sortied repeatedly to clear a way to the causeways, but the Mexica masses simply reoccupied in their rear the houses the Spanish had already cleared. The Spanish were always forced to fight their way back into their compound. The Indians fought for every building, even the women joining in, hurling stones from their roofs. Everywhere the canals, their bridges removed, blocked the Spanish. Even a successful assault on the Great Temple lead by Cortés in person failed to demoralize the Mexica. Considering that in Mesoamerican warfare the firing of a city's main temple meant that the patron deity had been defeated, this attack was a stupendous statement of Mexica resolve to fight it out to the end.[19]

The next day, in desperation, Cortés sent to Motecuhzoma to ask him to again address his people from the roof and order them to desist. The messengers found him overwhelmed with grief and furious at his treatment. He said, "What more does Malinche want of me? I neither wish to live nor to listen to him, to such a pass has my fate brought me because of him." He then said he would not go to the roof and did not want to see Cortés or hear his lies again. Two of the Spanish leaders went to Motecuhzoma to beg him to help. Although cooped up in the compound, he had retained his sources of information. "I believe that I shall not obtain any result towards ending this war, for they have already raised up another Lord and have made up their minds not to let you leave this place alive, therefore I believe that all of you will have to die."[20]

Death of the Tlatoani: A Murder Mystery

Desperately they tried to convince him that they wanted to leave but could do so only if he could calm the Mexica. Reluctantly he agreed and climbed again to the roof. Perhaps he understood the nature of this last appearance; he clothed himself in the full regalia of the *tlatoani*. Attendants draped the blue and white checked mantle over his shoulders, held by a brilliant green *chalchiuitl* stone. Greenstone gems sparkled from his golden jewelry, and golden-soled sandals were on his feet. Finally he placed on his head the imperial turquoise Toltec diadem.

Thus attired and preceded by the golden wand of office and guarded by a group of shield-bearing Spaniards, he walked along the battlements. The noise of battle quickly died as he was recognized. Many of his warriors instinctively kissed earth or averted their gaze. The rest watched in expectant silence. His calm voice carried across the packed square.

Why do I see my people here in arms against the palace of my fathers? Is it that you think your sovereign a prisoner, and wish to release him? If so, you have acted rightly. But you are mistaken. I am no prisoner. The strangers are my guests. I remain with them only from choice, and can leave them when I list. Have you come to drive them from the city? That is unnecessary. They will depart of their own accord, if you will open a way for them. Return to your homes, then. Lay down your arms. Show your obedience to me who have a right to it. The white men shall go back to their own land; and all shall be well again within the walls of Tenochtitlan.[21]

Four Mexica captains came forward and spoke to him below the wall to tell him that they had elected his brother, Cuitláhuac, as the new *tlatoani*. They had pledged to Huitzilopochtli to fight the war to a finish. In these few moments, the import of Motecuhzoma's speech had sunk into the mass of his listeners. Rage shot through the vast crowd. The last tatters of respect for the *tlatoani* evaporated, replaced by contempt for the man who had repeatedly betrayed his nation. The mass snarled in hate, throwing once unthinkable insults up to the man on the battlements.

Through the noise, a clear, strong voice sounded like a trumpet. It was Cuauhtémoc: "What is that which is being said by that scoundrel of a Motezuma, whore of the Spaniards? Does he think that he can call to us, with his woman-like soul, to fight for the empire which he has abandoned out of fright. . . . We do not want to obey him because already he is no longer our monarch and, indeed, we must give him the punishment which we give to a wicked man."[22]

Then the snarls turned to action. Hands that held bows, stones, or *atlatls* now used them. It was said that the first dart thrown at him was from the hand of Cuauhtémoc. Motecuhzoma's bodyguards had dropped their shields at the crowd's initial silence and were unprepared for the rain of missiles that now fell on the party on the wall. Motecuhzoma was struck with three stones and fell to the parapet. He was quickly rushed to his apartments. Only one stone, which struck him in the head, was said to have caused serious injury, but perhaps the anger in the stone was more deadly than the substance. In any case, he simply wanted to die. He tore off the bandages and refused to be treated. From absolute monarch he had allowed himself to become the prisoner of an enemy, then his puppet, and finally a tool in battle against his own people. This realization, which he had kept at bay for a long time, now crushed him more utterly than the stone. As Prescott would write in the nineteenth century, "He had survived his honor." Cortés and others came to encourage him in his recovery and to plead with him to accept baptism, but he remained silent and brooding. Soon after they returned to the fighting on 29 June, Motecuhzoma died.

Cortés's account in his second letter to Charles V was suspiciously terse for such a momentous event. "[He] received a blow on his head from a stone; and the injury was so serious that he died three days later. I told two of the Indians who were captive to carry him out on their shoulders to the people. What they did with him I do not know; only the war did not stop because of it, but grew more fierce and pitiless each day."[23] Díaz wrote that "when we least expected it, they came to say that he was dead. . . . At the end of much discussion Cortés ordered a priest and a chief from among the prisoners to go and tell the Cacique whom they had chosen for Lord who was named Cuitlahuac, and his Captains, that the great Montezuma was dead, and they had seen him die, and about the manner of his death and the wounds his own people had inflicted on him."

Cortés then ordered six nobles and the remaining priests held in captivity to go to Cuitláhuac and his captains. They were to carry him out of the compound on their shoulders and turn the body over to the Mexica. Díaz went on to say that the nobles had been present when Motecuhzoma died. "When they beheld him thus dead, we saw that they were in floods of tears and we clearly heard the shrieks and cries of distress that they gave for him. . . . The Mexica shouted back at the Spaniards that they need not concern themselves with the burial of Motecuhzoma. Instead they should worry about their own lives for they would be dead in two days. The Mexica had chosen a new leader who "would not be so faint-hearted as to be deceived with false speeches like their good Montezuma. . . . [W]ith these words they fell on us with loud yells and whistles and showers of stones, darts and arrows, while other squadrons were still attempting to set fire to our quarters in many places."[24]

The Indian accounts consistently claim the Spanish murdered Motecuhzoma. Durán's Indian informants insisted, even under his persistent questioning, that Motecuhzoma had survived his stoning, in fact that the wound was almost healed. After the Spaniards fled the city, the Mexica entered Motecuhzoma's apartment to kill him. They found him still shackled with five stab wounds in his body "and many chieftains and lords who had been imprisoned with him were all stabbed to death when they [the Spaniards] fled their quarters." Among these dead were Itzcuauhtzin, lord of Tlatelolco and Cacamatzin, lord of Texcoco. Durán's Indian sources stated that Cacamatzin fought so hard that he had to be brought down with 47 stab wounds."[25] Ixtlilxóchitl wrote that the Mexica palace servants attested that Motecuhzoma was stabbed to death by the Spaniards.[26] Sahagún's Indian informants are in substantial agreement, stating that Motecuhzoma and his suite were strangled and their bodies thrown over the palace roof to a place called "the Stone Turtle," for the carving there next to a canal.[27] Interestingly, there is a Spanish account that seems in part to support the Indian position. The conquistador, Francisco de Aguilar, was assigned as a guard for Motecuhzoma and the other prisoner lords. He wrote,

> Moctezuma, wounded in the head, gave up his soul to his Maker at about the hour of vespers. In the quarters where he was lodged there were other great lords being held with him, and with the approval of the captains Cortés had them killed, leaving not a single one. Later the bodies were removed and thrown in the porticos where the stores are now. Some of the Indians who had not been killed carried them out, and after night fell, at about ten o'clock, a terrifying mob of women appeared carrying torches and flaming braziers. They came for their husbands and relatives who lay dead in the porticos, and they came for Moctezuma, too. And as the women recognized their

men (which we could see, by the great amount of light, from the rooftop where we kept watch) they threw themselves upon them with great sorrow and grief, and raised such a wailing and screeching that it made one fearful. This writer, who was on guard duty, said to his companion: "Have you not seen the hell and flood of tears over there? For if you have not seen it, you may witness it from here." In truth, never in all the war and the difficulties I went through was I so afraid as when I saw that fearful lamentation.[28]

What is to be made of these inconsistencies? Cortés was not an absolute master of his expedition and often had to give in to the most brutal and fearful demands of his captains, against his better judgment. This may have been such an occasion. However, Cortés was also willing to take brutal actions when he thought necessary. Given the desperation of such men and their record of precipitate bad judgment, one need not seek further for motives. The murder of Motecuhzoma was not likely something Cortés would have advertised, nor would the small group of executioners have wanted to brag of it. Many of the common Spanish soldiers, including Díaz, may never have heard of the murders and believed Cortés's disingenuous account. Such an act of murder would not have been acceptable at the court in Madrid, where kingship was an exclusive club, and regicide never to be legitimized. Later in the century the king of Spain would imprison the former governor of Peru for executing the last Inca and his family, stating, "I did not send you to murder kings."[29]

Cortés was also willing to dissemble in his letters to the emperor. He made no mention of killing the other captured Mexica lords, including Cacamatzin, despite the testimony of Aguilar, who had been their jailer. Instead he claimed three times that they had been killed in the retreat from Tenochtitlan shortly after. Perhaps that was a case of protesting too much. Díaz states that Cacamatzin and the other lords were indeed killed in the retreat, but he was writing this forty years after the event and does not claim to have been an actual witness to any of the deaths.

Traditional scholarship finds the murder of Motecuhzoma improbable, despite the assertions from a number of Indian or *mestizo* sources. Those sources, however, should not be lightly dismissed as the bitterness of a conquered people. If modern scholarship cites the firsthand accounts of the conquistadors, then it should give equal weight to the native sources. The native sources of Durán and Sahagún were also contemporaries. In addition, Durán based much of his history on the now lost *Chrónica X*, the official Mexica history.[30]

"He Terrorized the World"

Díaz wrote that upon the news of Motecuhzoma's death, "Cortés wept for him, and all of us Captains and soldiers, and there was no man among us who knew him and was intimate with him, who did not bemoan him as though he was our father, and it is not to be wondered at, considering how good he was."[31] Of course, they would have thought of him so. He had been a constant source of wealth to them and had done everything in his power to ingratiate himself with them. As we have seen, however, his people had a far different impression of their traitor *tlatoani.*

The traditional funeral of a *tlatoani* was ignored; his body was simply cremated. As Sahagún's Indian informants wrote, "The fire crackled, seeming to flare up, to send up many tongues of flame; many tongues of flame, many sprigs of flame seemed to rise. And Moctezuma's body seemed to lie sizzling, and it smelled foul as it burned." The people cried out in their anger, cursing him even in death: "This blockhead! He terrorized the world; there was dread in the world, there was astonishment. This man! If anyone offended him only a little, he at once disposed of him. Many he punished for imagined [faults] which were not real, which were only a fabrication of words."[32]

His subjects in their vengeance sought out his wives and children and killed all they could find. Surely they thought of the description of the bad ruler, of which the last words—"He is wished dead"—had surely come to pass.

The Dusk of Empire

Even as his corpse grew cold, Motecuhzoma's dead hand held the fate of the Mexica in its grip. The damage he had done to the empire had left it too narrow a margin in the dangerous days that were to follow. There were only a few chances to recover the situation. One by one they would be missed.

The Toxcatl massacre had cut a deadly swath through the Mexica governing and military elites. It would be experience that the Mexica would miss, not courage. This they demonstrated repeatedly in the week that the Spaniards stood desperate siege in their palace compound.

The new *tlatoani* at least provided the mature leadership the Mexica needed. Cuitláhuac quickly organized a winning strategy—relentless assaults by overwhelming mass. Again and again the Spaniards sortied from their compound hoping to carve a way out of the city, only to be hemmed in and driven back by countless Mexica and their allies. The city itself, with its canals and buildings, was an impossible barrier for the Spaniards. The Mexica squadrons were stacked up along the causeways, waiting their turn. Cuitláhuac boldly told Cortés that he would trade casualties twenty-five to one to destroy the Spaniards. Nothing Cortés could do would sway Cuitláhuac from this objective, neither feats of arms nor ploys of negotiation.

In desperation, Cortés and his officers decided to risk a dash for the Tlacopan causeway in the dead of night just after midnight on 30 June. A portable bridge was fashioned from great roof timbers to be placed over each canal, then brought forward to the next canal. Luck favored the Spaniards that night; a torrential rainstorm drove the Mexica sentries indoors, a lapse of discipline that can only be explained by the massacre of the military elite, as well as the Mexica reluctance to fight at night. The head of the Spanish column reached the edge of the causeway before the alarm was given.

The city sprang to arms, and masses of warriors fell upon the column from every direction. The bridge became stuck at the Toltec Canal, to be forever known thereafter as the Bridge of Massacre. A fleet of canoes threw warriors directly into the panicked column on the causeway. It was every man for himself as the Mexica took their revenge. Cortés was unhorsed and swarmed over by Mexica eager for the greatest prize of all, but his companions fought him free. So great was the disaster that fewer than four hundred Spaniards and two thousand Tlaxcallans got through to limp into the city of Tlacopan. As many as a thousand Spaniards and four thousand Tlaxcallans had perished or been taken captive to die on the stone of sacrifice. Forgotten among the dead were a son, Chimalpopoca, and two daughters of Motecuhzoma, one of them the young Doña Anna, pregnant by Cortés. The Spaniards would forever call this disaster *la Noche Triste*, the Sad Night.[1]

To the amazement of the survivors, there was no pursuit. The famous Mexica discipline broke down in an orgy of looting on the causeway. The arms, armor, and stolen treasures of the Spaniards were irresistible. There were too few experienced Mexica captains to bring order to such chaos. Had the Mexica pursued their enemy, Tlacopan would have been the last stand. As it was, Cuitláhuac had inflicted the greatest defeat and heaviest losses on a European army in the conquest of the Americas.

But the fruits of victory are gathered in the pursuit, and that was slow in coming. Cortés, for his part, wasted no time putting his exhausted force on the road, heading northward around Lake Texcoco for the safety of Tlaxcallan. The pursuit had been slow but eventually Cuitláhuac intercepted Cortés on 8 July at Otumba, in the northeastern part of the Valley of Mexico. The Mexica had come across the lake in canoes to be joined by their junior partners in the Triple Alliance, the men of Texcoco and their vassals.

The Mexica commanded a large but brittle host. The Texcocans made up the larger part of the force facing Cortés, but their internal divisions made them unsteady. Cortés had sown much dissension in that kingdom in the preceding six months, by favoring Ixtlilxóchitl, the rebel prince. Many in Texcoco favored Ixtlilxóchitl. Motecuhzoma's failure either to destroy or co-opt Ixtlilxóchitl now weakened the Triple Alliance at the decisive moment. There was disarray in the Mexica ranks as well—more evidence of the loss of experienced leaders at Toxcatl. For some reason, Cuitláhuac did not command in person at Otumba, having given command to the *Cihuacoatl.*

Still, the Spanish position seemed hopeless. Every man was wounded and exhausted. Their cannon and firearms had been lost. Only five men remained mounted. The Mexica and Texcocans came at them in waves, each replaced as it tired. Despite the desperate resistance, defeat of the Spanish seemed only a matter of time—until Cortés and the other four horsemen charged through the enemy ranks, straight at the *Cihuacoatl.* Amid all that brightly colored host, *Cihuacoatl,* riding in a litter, could be distinguished by a magnificent gold and green Quetzal feather banner, the Mexica national standard, strapped to his back. Cortés's horse slammed into the litter, hurling the Mexica from it; another horseman speared the *Cihuacoatl,* retrieved the banner, and gave it to Cortés. The conquistador rode through the Mexica ranks waving the banner aloft. Killing the enemy leader and taking his banner would have been a severe blow in a European battle; here it was a disaster for his enemy. Cortés had no idea, but the Indians believed that Huitzilopochtli himself dwelled in the banner when it was carried to war. Cortés had seized the Hummingbird! The Mexica and Texcocans fled the field. The path to Tlaxcallan was open.

The Spaniards rested in the land of their allies, receiving rein-forcements and supplies. Through a subtle diplomacy Cortés con-tinued to undermine the bonds of fear that held the Mexica vassals. Cuitláhuac attempted to shore up his domestic front by marrying Tecuichpo, the favored and beautiful daughter of Motecuhzoma. It was a desperate thing to marry an eleven-year-old girl, even for po-litical purposes. He then sent rich embassies to the Tlaxcallans, of-fering them an equal place in the alliance and vast wealth. But again Motecuhzoma had done his work too well. His relentless wars and economic blockade had created such bitterness that Cuitláhuac's offers were rejected out of hand. Motecuhzoma had welded Tlaxcallan to the Spaniards. Requests that descended to begging also failed to bring the Tarascans to the aid of the Mexica.

Then another disaster befell the Mexica. A black slave with Narváev's expedition had brought smallpox to Mexico. He left a trail of the disease on his journey to Tenochtitlan and died in the fighting in the city. The smallpox arrived first in Chalco, at the southern end of the valley, and exploded with catastrophic effect in late October. By the end of December the storm had struck Tenochtitlan; it raged for sixty days, killing 30 to 40 percent of the population, as many as 120,000 people. It killed millions that year throughout central Mexico.[2] The timing for Cortés could not have been better. He marched into Anáhuac with a new army of six hundred Spaniards and twenty thousand Tlaxcallans on 28 De-cember, just as the smallpox paralyzed the city. One of the first to die was Cuitláhuac, who died on 3 January 1521. He had reigned barely eighty days. With him died many veteran warriors and leaders. Smallpox ripped Mexica society apart. Even on a simple organizational level, it was a catastrophe. The entire hierarchy of the society was disrupted. Countless vacant positions of authority had to be filled by new and inexperienced men. The subsequent resistance of the Mexica is all the more heroic in this light.

The electors of the decimated Eagle Clan chose the young Cuauhtémoc to succeed Cuitláhuac. Smallpox still raged in the city; his coronation was postponed until 21 February. One of his first acts was to execute at least one of Motecuhzoma's sons, Axo-cacatzin, and possibly several more, who urged reconciliation with Cortés and a softer line toward Christianity. He also found time to marry their sister, the young widow, Tecuichpo, the second of Motecuhzoma's daughters he had wed. In one way or another, Cuauhtémoc was thoroughly enmeshed in the family of Motecuhzoma.

Almost immediately after Cortés's arrival in Anáhuac, Texcoco, the second pillar of the Triple Alliance, fell, sending a wave of refugees into Tenochtitlan. The fighting came closer and closer to Tenochtitlan in the coming months as Cortés reduced city after city. Cuauhtémoc had his victories, but they were few and ultimately ephemeral. The young *tlatoani* tried repeatedly to adapt Spanish techniques and weapons, but the learning curve was too steep. The Mexica had captured hundreds of steel swords but had learned neither the lethal Spanish art of swordsmanship nor the disciplined machinelike tactic of fighting in ranks. Cortés's rain of blows gave the Mexica no time to experiment and adapt. By 20 May he had thrown Tenochtitlan itself under siege. His force had grown to over nine hundred Spaniards and almost a hundred thousand Indian allies.

When Cortés finally reached the city, Cuauhtémoc decided to stake everything on breaking Cortés quickly on its defenses of the city and the strength of its warriors. He had driven off three Spanish forays already as they neared the city, which gave him confidence in his ability to repel the besiegers. He relied entirely on this strategy and was not prepared to withstand a lengthy siege, something very rare in Mesoamerican military experience. This may explain his failure to provision the city properly. Although a young man with a young man's receptivity to new ideas, he was still a creature of a world ruled by a strict etiquette of war and honor. His misfortune was to be opposed by men possessed of a violent and adaptive flexibility and relentless drive.

In the weeks that followed, Cortés attacked down the causeways and broke into the city proper. Finding that fighting in a heavily built up city was fruitless, he ordered his Indian allies to demolish the city as the fighting moved forward and use the debris to fill in the canals. He was creating fields of fire for his cannons and firearms and flat ground for the cavalry. At the same time, he deprived the Mexica of the natural defenses of the city.

Cuauhtémoc in his own way was as obdurate as Cortés. He was an inspiring and ruthless leader who rallied his people to repeated acts of heroism and resolution. He had long ago cast his lot with Huitzilopochtli, who continued to promise victory. He would fight it out to the end. But nothing he could do halted the slow destruction of his city and the decimation of its population. Starvation filled the houses with corpses, and Cortés's Indian allies killed every Mexica that fell into their hands. Cortés would write of the scene as his allies slaughtered forty thousand Mexica noncombatants, "So loud was the wailing of the women and children that there was not one man amongst us whose heart did not bleed at the sound; and indeed we had more trouble in preventing our allies from killing with such cruelty than we had in fighting the enemy. For no race has practiced such fierce and unnatural cruelty as the native of these parts."[3] He would estimate later that at least another fifty thousand Mexica died from starvation and bad water.

Eventually, Tenochtitlan itself had to be abandoned as the surviving population moved en masse to its sister city of Tlatelolco. By early August, the Mexica were crowded into the surviving one-seventh of their city. Cuauhtémoc had completely lost control; the Mexica polity simply broke down. The Eagle Council and the *Cihuacoatl* surrendered on 13 August. With all lost, Cuauhtémoc fled the city the same day with his family by canoe. Captured by a Spanish brigantine, Cuauhtémoc was escorted to Cortés by three Spanish captains holding tightly to his mantle. Cuauhtémoc's bearing did not desert him even at this moment. Cortés told Marina, his interpreter, "Ask Cuauhtémoc why he permitted the destruction of the city with such loss of lives of his own people and of ours? Many were the times that I begged him for peace."

Cuauhtémoc answered, "Tell the captain that I have done my duty; I have defended my city, my kingdom just as he would have defended his had I attempted to take it from him. But I have failed!" He then put his hand on Cortés's dagger at his belt. "Now that I am his captive, let him take this dagger and kill me with it!"[4]

He and the other surviving lords were escorted to Coyohuacan under careful guard. That night the heavens opened in a great deluge that rocked the valley and pounded the ruins of Tenochtitlan to their foundations. "It seemed as if the deities of Anáhuac, scared from their ancient abodes, were borne along shrieking and howling in the blast, as they abandoned the fallen capital to its fate." [5] Cuauhtémoc's thoughts were still with the tormented survivors, and he quickly begged Cortés to allow them to flee the charnel-house ruins and find refuge around the lake shore.

Cortés, the admirer of chivalrous legends, was much affected by this act of heroic nobility. He quickly assented and assured Cuauhtémoc both of his safety and that he, Cortés, esteemed him all the more for his courage. He had Cuauhtémoc's family brought and provided with the best food in the camp. He also promised to confirm Cuauhtémoc in his own authority. Then he escorted the Mexica to a rooftop, pointed at the scene of desolation and turmoil before them, and begged him to order the last of his warriors, still huddled on rooftops, to surrender. Cuauhtémoc raised his arms, and the war was over.

The Indian allies still ignored orders to spare the survivors, so Cortés encouraged them to go home, which they happily did, laden with loot. An estimated 240,000 Mexica and thirty thousand Texcocans had perished in the siege. [6] For the next three days, through the continuing downpour, the last 150,000 of the Mexica, emaciated and haggard, trudged out of the corpse-stuffed rubble heap that once had been one of the jewels of the planet. Some of them stopped from time to time to gaze back upon the bones of their city.

Cortés's chivalry, however, had its limits. Now, instead of Tlaxcallan barbarities, they suffered Spanish greed. Women were stripped to find any gold hidden on them. Young men were branded for slavery, and comely, light-skinned young women carried off. Spanish mastiffs were set upon the priests to tear them to pieces. Where once the mighty twin cities of Tenochtitlan and Tlatelolco had stood there was now "the plain of Cortés," where not even a stick stood upright. There was also the matter of the gold lost on *la Noche Triste*. To Cortés's rage, Cuauhtémoc could produce little. Cortés yielded to pressure from the royal treasurer to torture the gold out of the Mexica lords. Cuauhtémoc and Tetlepanquetzatzin, king of Tlacopan, were tied to poles, and their feet were covered with oil and set alight. Tetlepanquetzatzin, in agony, watched for a sign from the impassive Cuauhtémoc that he would say something that would stop the torture. But Cuauhtémoc only glared at him, calling him weak and cowardly: "And do you think, I, then, am taking my pleasure in my bath?"[7] All he would admit was that when defeat was certain, he had had the gold all thrown into the deepest part of the lake.

Cuauhtémoc survived this treatment and for the next four years remained titular *tlatoani* of the Mexica. However, it was to the *Cihuacoatl,* Tlacotzin, grandson of the great Tlacaélel, that Cortés entrusted the rebuilding of the city. It was Tlacotzin who conveyed to Cortés the matter-of-fact attitude with which the Mexica now accepted the Conquest. It was the way of the world— "The Mexica had no lands when we [the Mexica] first came here; the Tepaneca, the Acolhua, the Chalca, and the Xochimilca, all had lands. We took their lands. But what we did was no different from what you have done, our lord, for you came with arrows and shields to take our lands and cities from us."

Cortés, who still feared that Cuauhtémoc might hatch a plot, kept him within calling distance at all times. In 1525 he ordered Cuauhtémoc to accompany him on an expedition to Honduras. During that campaign Cortés accused him of plotting a revolt and swiftly pronounced a sentence of death. As Cuauhtémoc was led to the ceiba tree from which he was to be hanged, he said to Cortés, "I knew what it was to trust to your false promises, Malinche; I knew that you had destined me to this fate, since I did not fall by my own hand when you entered my city of Tenochtitlan. Why do you slay me so unjustly? God will demand it of you!"[8]

In a complete break with Mexica tradition, Cortés chose Tlacotzin to succeed Cuauhtémoc, but the new *tlatoani* lived but a year. The next two rulers were not of the Eagle Clan and were not given the title of *tlatoani.* In 1542 the royal line was restored, as grandsons of Axayácatl and Tizoc took the throne. The last of the royal line died in 1563, and as the Indian chronicler lamented, "Thus ended the rule of the sons of the much-loved kings of the Tenochca in Mexico-Tenochtitlan." By then the substance of Indian rule had long been only a shadow of the splendor and might of Motecuhzoma's day.[9]

Many of Motecuhzoma's numerous children had not survived the fall of the empire. However, two of his children by Teotalco were destined to mingle with bluest blood in Europe. After Cuauhtémoc's death, Motecuhzoma's favorite daughter, the beautiful Tecuichpo, took the name of Isabel de Moctezuma and married three conquistadors in succession, the last of whom was Juan Cano. Between these husbands, she managed to have a daughter by Cortés. Her descendants by Cano are found today in a score of the noble houses of Spain and France.

Tlacahuepan, a natural son of Motecuhzoma, assumed the name of Don Pedro de Moctezuma. His grandson was given the title of Count of Moctezuma in 1627; the Spanish throne advanced the title to that of the Duke of Moctezuma in 1865. The current holder of the title is Don Juan Jose Marcilla de Teruel Moctezuma y Jimenez, fifth Duque de Moctezuma and Grande de España, who acceded to the title in 1991.

A third child, who took the name Francesca, would have a son, Fernando Alvarado Tezozomoc, who would not number European nobility among his descendants but, having inherited the surviving books of the royal family, would be one of the great historians of the vanished world of his Mexica ancestors.

What of the Hummingbird? After Cuitláhuac's death, the idol was removed for safekeeping to Azcapotzalco. During the siege of Tenochtitlan, it was closer to Cortés's camp than to Cuauhtémoc's palace. For the next quarter-century, the Catholic clergy pursued it with great fervor from place to place. In the end, the Hummingbird eluded them. He remains today wrapped in his carrying bundle, reputedly sealed in a cave near the ancient Tollan of the Toltecs, still awaiting restoration.[10]

Epilogue

M

OTECUHZOMA MAY HAVE DIED on the day the Spaniards fled Tenochtitlan, but his ghost continued to haunt the Mexica. His successors would be crippled by the consequences of his reign. Other men would don the turquoise Toltec diadem as *tlatoani*. They would be men of heroic stature, in the mold of the best of their empire-building ancestors. But none could escape the train of events that Motecuhzoma had set in motion from the moment he came to power in 1502.

Ironically, on the fateful day in the year 1-Reed, when Cortés arrived, the Mexica Empire outwardly seemed to be at its apogee of wealth, extent, and power. Beneath the splendor, however, was a fateful brittleness. The empire had always been vulnerable, as all such vassal-based empires have been, but strong, clear-eyed, and determined leadership had consistently masked that weakness. Motecuhzoma had collapsed the moral center of the empire from within, leaving only the seemingly awesome shell intact.

At three levels Motecuhzoma fundamentally weakened the empire. The first two levels were in place prior to the arrival of the Spaniards.

His reorganization of the state had made for great imperial theatrics but had induced a level of rigidity and lack of initiative that would ultimately deprive the Mexica of the flexibility to respond effectively to the Spanish invasion. In effect, by centralizing power in his own person and assuming the attributes of a god, he cut himself off from good counsel. This was a direct repudiation of the system the Eagle Clan had so successfully employed in the past. He also made it suicidal for subordinates to take any initiative without direct orders from the imperial center.

Second, his self-identification with Huitzilopochtli was perhaps a logical progression in Mexica imperial history. By assuming aspects of the godhead and by championing Huitzilopochtli against the rest of the pantheon, he created a level of religious dissension in Anáhuac that weakened loyalty to the center among vassal elites. His support of the power of the priesthood against other interests also weakened the ability of the Mexica to respond to a new and extraordinary threat.

Finally, his unreasoning enmity to the Enemies of the House created ready-made allies for the Spaniards. It was the Enemies of the House, particularly Tlaxcallan, which gave Cortés the secure base and the large number of first-class fighting men necessary to subdue the Mexica.

All of these wounds, however, could not have been so fully exploited by Cortés had Motecuhzoma not simply lost his nerve in the face of the unexpected. It was Motecuhzoma's moral collapse that undid the empire. His rigid personality demanded utter control of his environment. When he could no longer exert that control, he fell to pieces. Admittedly, the arrival of the Spaniards was a profound event, but it was made fatal by Motecuhzoma's fundamental personality flaw. It is difficult to believe that practical and ruthless men like Motecuhzoma I and Ahuítzotl would have responded so supinely. Surely ancient Tlacaélel, the creator of the imperial cult of Huitzilopochtli, would not have failed to see exactly what the Spaniards were. All of these men would have reacted aggressively to destroy the Europeans. Even Motecuhzoma's closest advisers in the Eagle Council, his own brother Cuitláhuac and his nephew Cuauhtémoc, recognized the danger immediately and recommended appropriate action. Cacamatzin, who initially agreed with Motecuhzoma about admitting the Spaniards into

Tenochtitlan, quickly recognized the error and tried to organize resistance.

Instead, Motecuhzoma turned over the empire as a running concern to the Spaniards. The Mexica Empire cracked at its foundation at the moment when Motecuhzoma and Cortés met on the causeway at Xoloc. At one stroke he severed the bonds of fear upon which the empire had been built—he admitted the existence of a greater earthly power and surrendered sovereignty to it. When Cortés and his toughs came to seize him in his own palace, even his physical courage failed him. He even offered his own children in his place.

Next he failed to defend Huitzilopochtli and thereby made nonsense of the Mexica imperial idea that Tlacaélel had so carefully constructed for over sixty years. When Cortés leapt into the air to smash the iron bar across the face of Hummingbird's idol, he challenged the god's invincibility. Motecuhzoma let that challenge stand.

Finally, he betrayed his own subjects repeatedly to the Spaniards even when they had followed his orders, as in the case of the unfortunate Quauhpopoca, who perished at the stake for his obedience. He also actively helped Cortés crush an attempt by the leading men of the empire to destroy the Spaniards; the Mexica leadership was effectively decapitated when Cuitláhuac, Cacamatzin, and others were arrested and chained in the palace. His last and most pathetic betrayal was on the rooftop of his father's own palace. He begged his own enraged people, seething over the massacre of Toxcatl, to return to their obedience to the Spaniards, declaring that they, and not the Mexica, were invincible. Their response came in a hail of darts, arrows, and sling stones. The Mexica had rejected him utterly but too late, too late. He had already sealed their doom.

Notes

Preface

1. The name "Aztec" is derived from their place of origin—Atzlan. On their journey, their deity ordered them to change their name to "Mexica." After the Conquest, when their history was studied, the name Aztec was revived and applied to all the Náhuatl-speaking inhabitants of Central Mexico.

Chapter 1

1. Richard F. Townsend, *The Aztecs,* rev. ed. (London: Thames and Hudson, 2000), 65.

2. The name "Cihuacoatl" is that of a goddess; the title probably originated as a priestly office.

3. R. C. Padden, *The Hummingbird and the Hawk: Conquest and Sovereignty in the Valley of Mexico 1503-1541* (New York: Harper and Row, 1967), 6–7. In their southward migration, the Mexica passed through the land of the Tarascans in Michoacán. The Tarascan primary deity was a hummingbird, its name, *tzinzuni,* yielded the Náhuatl word *huitzilin,* to which was added *opochtli,* meaning "on the left." In Mesoamerica right and left signified north and south. The Mexica had learned of the cult as they passed south through the land of the Tarascans before entering the Valley of Mexico. In their days of empire the Mexica would import green hummingbird feathers from Michoacán to adorn the idol of Huitzilopochtli. This "aura of divinity" was later attached to a strong leader whose memory evolved into a hero cult and then a divinity. Additionally, the hummingbird image had a consistently fixed association with sacrifice in Mesoamerica.

4. Nigel Davies, *The Aztecs* (Norman: University of Oklahoma Press, 1989), 125.

5. Frances Gillmor, *The King Danced in the Marketplace* (Tuscon: University of Arizona Press, 1964), 10–11.

6. Diego Durán, *The History of the Indies of New Spain,* trans. Doris Heyden and Fernando Horcasitas (New York: Orion, 1964), 184–85.

7. Bernal Díaz del Castillo, *The Discovery and Conquest of Mexico* (New York: Farrar, Straus and Cudahy, 1956), 217.

8. Durán (p. 199) insists that the figure of 80,400 is accurate, having checked numerous other Indian sources in "written and painted manuscripts." This figure has generated one of the great controversies of Mexican history. Many prominent historians scoff at the figure as an administrative impossibility, simply from the perspective of body disposal. The Nazis also found body disposal a serious problem, in the death camps; however, it was not a problem that was allowed to interfere with the killing.

9. Ibid., 199.

10. Tezozomoc, "Crónica Mexicayótl," *Anales de Museo de Arqueologia, Historia y Etnografia,* epcoa 4, vol. 5 (1927), 333; Jonathan Kandell, *La Capital: The Biography of Mexico City* (New York: Henry Holt, 1989), 54.

11. Tezozomoc, 384.

12. Neil Baldwin, *Legends of the Plumed Serpent: Biography of a Mexican God* (New York: Public Affairs, 1998), 39.

Chapter 2

1. Diego Durán, *The History of the Indies of New Spain,* trans. Doris Heyden and Fernando Horcasitas (New York: Orion, 1964), 220.

2. Ibid.

3. R. C. Padden, *The Hummingbird and the Hawk: Conquest and Sovereignty in the Valley of Mexico 1503–1541* (New York: Harper and Row, 1970), 79.

4. Fray Bernadino de Sahagún, *The Florentine Codex,* Book 10, *The People,* Part XI (Salt Lake City: University of Utah Press, 1961), 15.

5. *Codex Ramírez* (Mexico City: Editorial Leyenda, 1944), 97; quoted in Davies, *The Aztecs,* 209.

6. *Codex Ramírez*, 97–98, quoted in Davies, 214.

7. Davies, *The Aztecs*, 97–98.

8. Durán, 215.

9. Ibid., 215–16.

10. Ibid., 224.

11. Padden, 11.

12. There is an interesting parallel with the way Mohammed elevated the patron deity of his Koresh tribe, Allah, the Arabian moon god, one among many in the pagan Arab pantheon, into the only god.

13. Ixtlilxochitl, *Historia*, caps. lxxi–lxxii, cited in Padden, 89.

14. Tezozómoc, Hernando Alvarado, *Crónica Mexicana* (Mexico City: Editorial Leyenda, 1944), 402; in Davies, 213.

15. C. A. Burland, *Montezuma: Lord of the Aztecs* (New York: G. P. Putnam's Sons, 1973), 149–50.

16. Davies, 217.

17. Ibid., 228.

18. William H. Prescott, *History of The Conquest of Mexico* (Philadelphia: J. B. Lippincott, 1873), 2: 82; Burland, 146; Hernan Cortés, *Letters from Mexico*, ed. and trans. Anthony Pagden (New Haven, Conn.: Yale University Press, 1986), 109.

19. Burland, 119, 121, 126.

20. Cortés, 110–11.

21. Ibid., 112.

Chapter 3

1. Diego Durán, *The History of the Indies of New Spain*, trans. Doris Heyden and Fernando Horcasitas (New York: Orion, 1964), 237. Durán describes the *Cihuacoatl* as the commander in this campaign or at least the part that marched on Tzotzollan. In any case, Motecuhzoma would rarely command his armies in person in the future.

2. Ross Hassig, *Aztec Warfare: Imperial Expansion and Political Control* (Norman: University of Oklahoma Press, 1988), 230.

3. Durán, 232.

4. Ibid., 242.

5. Hassig, 234–35.

Chapter 4

1. Diego Durán, *The History of the Indies of New Spain*, trans. Doris Heyden and Fernando Horcasitas (New York: Orion, 1964), 241.

2. Ibid., 467.

3. Fray Bernadino de Sahagún, *The Florentine Codex,* Book 10, *The People,* Part XI (Salt Lake City: University of Utah Press, 1961).

4. Durán, 258.

5. Hugh Thomas, *Conquest: Montezuma, Cortés, and the Fall of Old Mexico* (New York: Simon and Schuster, 1993), 184.

6. *Codex Chimalpopoca,* trans. J. Bierhorst, in *Four Masterworks of American Indian Literature* (Tucson: University of Arizona Press, 1974), 37; cited in Thomas, 184.

7. Durán, 264.

8. Sahagún, Book 12, *The Conquest of Mexico,* 17–18.

9. Ibid., 20.

10. Durán, 275.

11. Sahagún, Book 12, 26.

12. Ibid., 30.

13. Thomas, 270. Thomas suggests that the sorcerers were experiencing the hallucinogenic effects of sacred mushrooms.

Chapter 5

1. Diego Durán, *The History of the Indies of New Spain,* trans. Doris Heyden and Fernando Horcasitas (New York: Orion, 1964), 287.

2. Francisco López Gómora, *Cortés: The Life of the Conqueror by His Secretary,* ed. and trans. Lesley Byrd Simpson (Berkeley: University of California Press, 1964), 138.

3. William H. Prescott, *The History of the Conquest of Mexico,* 3 vols. (Philadelphia: J. B. Lippincott, 1873), 2: 82–83.

4. Ibid., 71–72.

5. Fray Bernadino de Sahagún, *The Florentine Codex,* Book 12, *The Conquest of Mexico* (Salt Lake City: University of Utah Press, 1961), 44. The sources are divided about when Motecuhzoma delivered this speech. The Indian sources of Sahagún and Durán place it at the bridge, but Cortés placed it later in the day after they had been shown to their quarters in the palace of Axayácatl. I have relied on the Indian sources here, suspecting that Motecuhzoma was probably anxious to relate what weighed so heavily upon him and would have done so on the causeway when the two sat to speak.

6. Ibid., 45.

7. Gómora, 140.

8. Hernán Cortés, *Letters from Mexico*, ed. and trans. Anthony Pagden (New Haven, Conn.: Yale University Press, 1986), 86.

9. Ibid., 85–86.

10. Ibid., 86.

11. Bernal Díaz de Castillo, *The Discovery and Conquest of New Spain* (New York: Farrar, Strauss, and Cudahy, 1956), 208.

12. Patricia de Fuentes, ed. and trans., *The Conquistadors: First-Person Accounts of the Conquest of Mexico* (Norman: University of Oklahoma Press, 1993), 147.

13. Díaz, 206.

14. Ibid., 221.

Chapter 6

1. Bernal Díaz de Castillo, *The Discovery and Conquest of New Spain* (New York: Farrar, Strauss, and Cudahy, 1956), 230.

2. Fray Bernadino de Sahagún, *The Florentine Codex,* Book 12, *The Conquest of Mexico* (Salt Lake City: University of Utah Press, 1961), 47.

3. Hernán Cortés, *Letters from Mexico*, ed. and trans. Anthony Pagden (New Haven, Conn.: Yale University Press, 1986), 90.

4. Díaz, 232.

5. Cortés, 97.

6. William H. Prescott, *The History of the Conquest of Mexico*, 3 vols. (Philadelphia: J. B. Lippincott, 1873), 2: 185

7. Ibid., 190

8. Cortés, 99.

9. Ibid., 99–100.

10. Díaz, 251.

Chapter 7

1. Andrés de Tapia, quoted in Patricia de Fuentes, ed. and trans., *The Conquistadors: First-Person Accounts of the Conquest of Mexico* (Norman: University of Oklahoma Press, 1993), 42–43.

2. Bernal Díaz de Castillo, *The Discovery and Conquest of New Spain* (New York: Farrar, Strauss, and Cudahy, 1956), 251–52.

3. Ibid., 252.

4. Tapia, 43–44.

5. R. C. Padden, *The Hummingbird and the Hawk: Conquest and Sovereignty in the Valley of Mexico 1503–1541* (New York: Harper Torch Books, 1967), 254.

6. Díaz, 252.

7. This festival was originally dedicated to Tetzcatlipoca, but it had tended instead to honor Huitzilopochtli—a good example of that latter's ascent to the top of the pantheon. His cult was in the process of shoving aside the ancient chief of the gods.

8. *Codex Aubin,* quoted in Miguel Leon-Portilla, *The Broken Spears: The Aztec Account of the Conquest of Mexico* (Boston: Beacon, 1992), 80–81.

9. Diego Durán, *The History of the Indies of New Spain,* trans. Doris Heyden and Fernando Horcasitas (New York: Orion, 1964), 297. Durán states that Cortés did so to set up the Mexica for massacre. Given Cortés's rage at Alvarado upon his return, this appears doubtful.

10. Inga Clendinnen, *The Aztecs* (Cambridge: Cambridge University Press, 1991), 115.

11. Fray Bernadino de Sahagún, *The Florentine Codex,* Book 12, *The Conquest of Mexico* (Salt Lake City: University of Utah Press, 1961), 55.

12. Durán, 298.

13. Sahagún, *Florentine Codex,* Book 12, 56.

14. Ibid.

15. Hugh Thomas, *Conquest: Montezuma, Cortés, and the Fall of Old Mexico* (New York: Simon and Schuster, 1993), 391.

16. Fray Bernadino de Sahagún, *Conquest of New Spain: 1585 Revision,* trans. Howard F. Cline (Salt Lake City: University of Utah Press, 1986), 79.

17. Sahagún, *Conquest of New Spain,* 107.

18. Díaz, 299.

19. Thomas, 402–403. Thomas contends the temple was actually that of Yopico, next to the palace of Axayácatl, rather than the Great Temple inside the Sacred Square. Given the limited range of Mexica missile weapons and the distance between the Great Temple and the palace of Axayácatl, he may be correct.

20. Díaz, 309.

21. William H. Prescott, *The History of the Conquest of Mexico* (Philadelphia: J. B. Lippincott, 1873), 2: 307.

22. *Codex Ramirez* (Mexico City: Editorial Leyenda, 1944), 147, quoted in Thomas, 401.

23. Hernán Cortés, *Letters from Mexico,* ed. and trans. Anthony Pagden (New Haven, Conn.: Yale University Press, 1986), 132.

24. Díaz, 310–11.

25. Durán, 305. Fernando de Alvarando de Tezozomac, *Chronica Mexicayotl* (Mexico City: Editorial Leyenda, 1949), identifies the two rulers also murdered as Motecuhzoma and Ixtlilxóchitl (2: 396). Cortés, 478, describes Cacamatzin's valiant end.

26. Fernando de Alva Ixtlilxóchitl, *Obras Historicas* (Mexico City: National University of Mexico, 1975–77), quoted in Miguel León-Portilla, *La Visión de los Vencidos* [The broken spears: The Aztec account of the conquest of Mexico] (Boston: Beacon, 1992), 90.

27. Sahagún, *Conquest of New Spain,* 85.

28. Fuentes, 154.

29. Cortés, 138–39, 176; Díaz, 317.

30. The *Chrónica X* and other codices used by these historians were amplified by the native mnemonic historians. The Náhuatl writing system was suited to accurate relation of hard facts, such as names, places, dates, numbers, etc., and general themes such as war, tribute, births, deaths, etc. It was not capable of word-for-word transmission. That was supplied by historians trained to extraordinary memory skills and able to remember exact words, prompted by the writing. Such historians amazed the Spanish chroniclers by reciting hour-long speeches over two hundred years old. Such mnemonic skills are far more highly developed in preliterate societies.

31. Díaz, 310.

32. Sahagún, *Florentine Codex,* Book 12, 65–66.

Chapter 8

1. Hernán Cortés, *Letters from Mexico,* ed. and trans. Anthony Pagden (New Haven, Conn.: Yale University Press, 1986), 139, 156.

2. Fray Bernadino de Sahagún, *Conquest of New Spain: 1585 Revision,* trans. Howard F. Cline (Salt Lake City: University of Utah Press, 1986), 103.

3. Cortes, 261–62.

4. Diego Durán, *The History of the Indies of New Spain,* trans. Doris Heyden and Fernando Horcasitas (New York: Orion, 1964), 316.

5. William H. Prescott, *The History of the Conquest of Mexico* (Philadelphia: J. B. Lippincott, 1873), 3: 195.

6. Hugh Thomas, *Conquest: Montezuma, Cortés, and the Fall of Old Mexico* (New York: Simon and Schuster, 1993), 528.
7. Ibid., 546.
8. Prescott, 3: 272–73; Francisco López de Gómora, *Cortés: The Life of the Conqueror by His Secretary,* ed. and trans. Lesley Byrd Simpson (Berkeley: University of California Press, 1964), 356. Gómora largely repeats Cortés's story but does not fail to condemn his actions, arguing that "Cortés, indeed, should have preserved his life as a precious jewel, for Cuauhtémoc was the triumph and glory of his victories; but Cortés did not want to keep him alive in such a troubled land and time."
9. Nigel Davies, *The Aztecs* (Norman: University of Oklahoma Press, 1989), 295.
10. R. C. Padden, *The Hummingbird and the Hawk: Conquest and Sovereignty in the Valley of Mexico 1503–1541* (New York: Harper Torch Books, 1967), 254–55, 270.

Bibliographic Note

THE SURVIVING NATIVE SOURCES on the history of Mesoamerica are magnificent but lonely. Almost all native books in existence were destroyed after the Conquest by the Spaniards, who believed they were an impediment to the hispanization of the Indians. Of course, the infamous Tlacaélel was also an imperial book burner, but his reach was more focused and not as great. The native sources that speak to us are essentially post-Conquest writings based on now-lost original sources.

Among the native sources that stand out is the *Anales de Tlatelolco,* which is the first work written using Náhuatl in Latin letters, probably 1524–28. It has been brilliantly adapted by Miguel León-Portilla, *La Visión de los Vencidos* [*The broken spears: The Aztec account of the conquest of Mexico*] (Boston: Beacon, 1992). León-Portilla has also produced an enchanting compilation of other native sources: *Pre-Columbian Literatures of Mexico* (Norman: University of Oklahoma Press, 1986). The grandson of Motecuhzoma II, Hernando Alvarado Tezozómoc, wrote in 1598 an account based on firsthand informants—*Crónica Mexicana* (Mexico City: Editorial Leyenda, 1944). *Crónica Mexicoyotl* (Mexico City: Editorial Leyenda, 1949) was a 1609 revision. Tezozómoc asserted his primary sources by identifying them as his mother, Doña Francisca de Motecuzoma, and his father, a Mexica of noble birth. He also had access to numerous other individuals who had lived before the Conquest, as well as now-vanished written native accounts. The chief among them appears to have been an original immediately post-Conquest Náhuatl chronicle, the lost *Crónica X,* which also apparently was a major primary source for other histories in the late sixteenth century.

The Dominican friar Fray Bernadino de Sahagún prepared one of the greatest ethnological studies in history, *The General History of the Things of New Spain* (Santa Fe, N. Mex.: School of American Research and the University of Utah, 1975), in thirteen books, also known as the *Florentine Codex,* of which Book 12 is *The Conquest of Mexico.* This study was based on the testimony, based on questionnaires, of committees of Indians who had lived through the Conquest. It was composed originally in Náhuatl then translated into Spanish and ultimately finished in 1576–77. The work covered not only the Conquest but also, in its other books, recorded the culture of the Náhuatl-speaking world in incredible detail. Sahagún revised Book 12 under official pressure so as to justify Spanish actions. See *Conquest of New Spain, 1585 Revision,* trans. Howard F. Cline (Salt Lake City: University of Utah Press, 1989).

Sahagún's effort was matched by his fellow friar, Fray Diego Durán, who had arrived in Mexico as a child and learned his Náhuatl from his playmates in Texcoco. His study was finished in 1581: *The Aztecs: The History of the Indies of New Spain,* trans. Doris Heyden and Fernando Horacasitas (New York: Orion, 1964); available in a revised edition as *The History of the Indies of New Spain,* trans. Doris Heyden (Norman: University of Oklahoma Press, 1994). Where Sahagún relied more on living informants, Durán employed native written sources, not only pre-Conquest codices but the rich post-Conquest Indian narratives and transcriptions of codices written in Náhuatl in Latin letters. It was said of Durán's work that "its main value is that it is the first and only chronicle of the sixteenth century that gives a harmonious view of Tenochtitlan." Durán also based much of his work on the lost *Crónica X.* This in turn may have been based on the official history of the Mexica commissioned by Tlacaélel himself and written down after the Conquest by a descendant, which may explain the ancient *Cihuacoatl's* prominence in Durán's

account. Durán's manuscript was sent to Spain after its comple-
tion and was not rediscovered, in the National Library of Madrid,
until 1854.

The Spanish accounts of their image of the Mesoamerican
world and their histories of the Conquest as used in this book rely
primarily on four works. Cortés himself wrote five letters to
Charles V of Spain during his expeditions—*Letters from Mexico*,
ed. and trans. Anthony Pagden (New Haven, Conn.: Yale University Press, 1986). Cortés provided an invaluable and often detailed
first-person narrative of events. His firsthand observations of
Motecuhzoma and the Indian world are some of the best we have.
However, it must be remembered that these letters had the primary purpose of justifying his disobedience of his orders from the
governor of Cuba and of portraying his actions in the best possible light. His secretary and chaplain, Francisco López de Gómora,
although not a participant in the Conquest, wrote a biography of
Cortés and first history of the Conquest in 1552, based upon the
Conquistador's personal accounts and records: *Cortés: The Life of
the Conqueror by His Secretary*, ed. and trans. Lesley Byrd Simpson
(Berkeley: University of California Press, 1964). This work should
be considered Cortés's *apologia pro vita sua*. The distance in time
gave Cortés the opportunity to offer a somewhat more balanced
view, yet one suspects that he still attempts to justify his actions.
Philip II, in any case, promptly suppressed the book for its irrev-
erent comments about his father, Charles V.

Another conquistador, Bernal Díaz de Castillo, wrote his
memoirs (*The Discovery and Conquest of New Spain* [New York:
Farrar, Strauss, and Cudahy, 1956]) in 1555 (and published in 1632)
in an attempt to counter many of the falsehoods he perceived in
Gómora's book. Though the space of thirty years had dimmed
some of the details of Díaz's work, it remains the finest memoir of
the Conquest and provides a wealth of detail found nowhere else
among the conquistadors with respect to the impression made on
the Spaniards by their entrance into the Mesoamerican world. It is
a wondrous book, well written with bold narrative that commu-
nicates with great immediacy the dangers, wonders, and deeds of
the Conquest. Other invaluable first-person accounts of the Conquest are found in the collection edited and translated by Patricia

de Feuntes: *The Conquistadors: First-person Accounts of the Conquest of Mexico* (Norman: University of Oklahoma Press, 1993).

Pride of place in the later histories of the Conquest falls to the great William H. Prescott, for his majesterial *The History of the Conquest of Mexico*, 3 vols. (Philadelphia: J. B. Lippincott, 1873). This magnificent history, first published in 1843, was the English-speaking world's first glimpse into the world of Mesoamerica, and it became a best seller. Its effect was amplified by the Mexican-American War, which began three years later and allowed thousands of American soldiers to see firsthand the scenes described so vividly by Prescott. It has lost none of its depth of scholarship, style, and drama today, after more than 160 years. Of the many editions of Prescott's history, the one illustrated by the magnificent drawings of Keith Henderson is a priceless visual feast: *The Conquest of Mexico* (London: Chatto and Windus, 1922). A worthy modern successor to Prescott is the well written and detailed account by Hugh Thomas, *Conquest: Montezuma, Cortés, and the Fall of Old Mexico* (New York: Simon and Schuster, 1993).

Mexica history is the realm of Nigel Davies (*The Aztecs* [Norman: University of Oklahoma Press, 1989] and *The Aztec Empire: The Toltec Resurgence* [Norman: University of Oklahoma Press, 1987]), Michael D. Coe (*Mexico: From the Olmecs to the Aztecs* [London: Thames and Hudson, 1994]), and Richard F. Townsend (*The Aztecs,* rev. ed. [London: Thames and Hudson, 1993]), whose interpretations are vital in making the native accounts of Sahagún and Durán fall into place. The rise and fall of the Toltec Empire and its successor states is also told by Davies (*The Toltecs: Until the Fall of Tula* [Norman: University of Oklahoma Press, 1987], and *The Toltec Heritage: From the Fall of Tula to the Rise of Tenochtitlan* [Norman: University of Oklahoma Press, 1980]). Of Motecuhzoma himself, there is the biography by C. A. Burland: *Montezuma: Lord of the Aztecs* (New York: G. P. Putnam's Sons, 1973).

The unchallenged authority on Aztec warfare and campaigns is Ross Hassig: *Aztec Warfare: Imperial Expansion and Political Control* (Norman: University of Oklahoma Press, 1988). Highly useful is volume 239 of the Osprey Men-At-Arms Series: John M. D. Pohl and Angus McBrige, *Aztec, Mixtec and Zapotec Armies* (London: Osprey, 1991).

Mesoamerican religion is treated in several fine works, of which two are Mary Miller and Karl Taube, *The Gods and Symbols of Ancient Mexico and the Maya: An Illustrated Dictionary of Mesoamerican Religion* (London: Thames and Hudson, 1993), and Roberta H. Markman and Peter T. Markman, *The Flayed God: The Mythology of Mesoamerica* (San Francisco: HarpersSanFranciso, 1993). In addition, Quetzalcoatl is the subject of Neil Baldwin's *Legends of the Plumed Serpent: Biography of a Mexican God* (New York: Public Affairs, 1998). R. C. Padden provides a fascinating account of the Huitzilopochtli cult: *The Hummingbird and the Hawk: Conquest and Sovereignty in the Valley of Mexico 1503–1541* (New York: Harper Torch Books, 1967).

Mexica culture is insightfully addressed by Miguel León-Portilla (*Aztec Thought and Culture* [Norman: University of Oklahoma Press, 1990]) and Inga Clendinnen (*Aztecs* [Cambridge: Cambridge University Press, 1993]).

Index

About the Author

Peter G. Tsouras is a distinguished defense analyst. For sixteen years previously he was a military intelligence analyst working for the U.S. Army on the military forces of the Soviet Union and Russia, Iran, and Iraq. He is also an accomplished writer of military history and alternate military history, having written or edited twenty-three books, including *Warlords of the Ancient Americas: Central America, Gettysburg: An Alternate History,* and *Alexander the Great: Invincible King of Macedonia.* He has had numerous television and radio interviews and has appeared in television documentaries as a commentator. He is married to the former Patricia Foley, has three children, and lives in Alexandria, Virginia.

MILITARY PROFILES
AVAILABLE

MILITARY PROFILES
FORTHCOMING

Halsey
Robert J. Cressman

Tirpitz
Michael Epkenhans

Petain
Robert B. Bruce

Winfield Scott
Samuel Watson

Benedict Arnold
Mark Hayes